REFLECTIONS ON OUR PASTC

Dexter Avenue Baptist Church, 1954–19(

CHAPLAIN LIEUTENANT COLONEL WALLY G. VAUGHN was born and reared in Sumter, South Carolina. He received a B.A. (History-Education) from Virginia Union University in 1976 and a Master of Divinity degree, School of Theology, Virginia Union University, in 1980. He received a Master of Theology degree from Princeton Theological Seminary in 1992.

In 1982, the National Baptist Convention, USA, Inc., endorsed him to serve as a chaplain in the United States Air Force. His assignments have included the Lowry Air Force Base, Colorado, Hahn AFB, Germany, McGuire AFB New Jersey, Operations Desert SHIELD/STORM, Air Force Institute of Technology (AFIT), Princeton Theological Seminary, Maxwell AFB Alabama, and the Royal Air Force, Mildenhall, England.

His military awards and decorations include: the Bronze Star Medal, Meritorious Service Medal (1 device), Air Force Commendation Medal (2 devices), Air Force Outstanding Unit Award (2 devices), Air Force Organizational Excellence Award, National Defense Medal, Southwest Asia Service Medal (2 devices), NATO Medal, Kuwait Liberation Medal (Saudi Arabian Government), and the Kuwait Liberation Medal (Kuwait).

He is the author of *From the Descent to the Exodus: Five Unresolved Issues*, a member of the National Baptist Convention, USA, Inc., and the Alpha Phi Alpha Fraternity, Inc.

He and his wife, the former Geraldine Hunt of Suffolk, Virginia, have two children: Wallisa and Wally, Jr.

REVEREND DR. RICHARD WAYNE WILLS was born in Saint Albans, New York. He has a B.S. in architecture from the New York Institute of Technology, Old Westbury, Long Island. He obtained a Master of Divinity with honors from the School of Theology, Virginia Union University. Reverend Wills earned a Doctor of Ministry Degree from the United Theological Seminary, Dayton, Ohio, in 1997.

Dr. Wills served as the pastor of Pilgrim Baptist Church, Richmond, Virginia, from October 1985 to July 1992. From August 1992 to December 1995 he served as the pastor at Dexter Avenue King Memorial Baptist Church, Montgomery, Alabama. Currently he is the assistant pastor of the Canaan Baptist Church of Christ, Harlem, New York—a position he assumed in January 1996.

Dr. Wills has held the position of Professor of Worship and Old Testament Studies at Selma University in Alabama. He has also been an

Adjunct Faculty member at the J. Sergeant Reynolds Community College, and the Richmond Technical Center, both in Richmond, Virginia.

Several community organizations have benefited from his membership. He has been the Southern Regional Director of the Clergy Support Team for OIC's of America, and an Executive Board Member of the Central Alabama OIC, the Montgomery United Way, the Montgomery Food Bank, the Montgomery Symphony, the Metro YMCA, Montgomery Improvement Association and the Hydea Foundation.

Dr. Wills is a member of the Progressive National Baptist Convention and the American Baptist Convention.

He is married to the former Sheila D. Martin of Lottsburg, Virginia, and they have four children: Richard Wayne, Jr., Reginald Dexter, Whitney Denise and Michele Sheila.

Reflections On Our Pastor Dr. Martin Luther King, Jr., at Dexter Avenue Baptist Church, 1954-1960

Wally G. Vaughn, Editor

Richard W. Wills, Assistant Editor

THE MAJORITY PRESS, INC.

Dover, Massachusetts

Library of Congress Cataloging-in-Publication Data
Reflections on our pastor : Dr. Martin Luther King, Jr., at
    Dexter Avenue Baptist Church, 1954-1960 / Wally
    G. Vaughn, Editor ; Richard
    W. Wills, asst. editor.
            p.   cm.
        Includes index.
        ISBN 0-912469-34-X
        1.   King, Martin Luther, Jr., 1929-1968. 2.
            Afro-American civil
        rights workers—United States—Biography. 3.
        Baptists—United
        States—Clergy—Biography. 4. Dexter Avenue
        Baptist Church
        (Montgomery, Ala.) 5. Afro-
        Americans—Alabama—Montgomery-
        •   Interviews. 6. Afro-
        Americans—Civil
        rights—Alabama—Montgomery—
        •   History--20th Century. 7.
        Montgomery (Ala.)—Race relations.
        8. Segregation in
        transportation—Alabama—Montgomery—Histo
        ry—20th
        century. I. Vaughn, Wally G., 1955-   . II.
        Wills, Richard W.,
        1956-   .
        E185.97.K5R45   1998
        323'.092—dc21
        [B]   98-19988
        CIP

        First published in 1999

    The Majority Press, Inc.
        PO Box 538
        Dover, MA 02030

        Printed in the United States of America

This book is dedicated to the memory of the late

Dr. and Mrs. Vernon Johns

PROGRAM OF INSTALLATION SERVICES

DEACON T. H. RANDALL, Presiding

Organ Prelude

Hymn No. 435

Invocation—Rev. John Porter

Anthem*

Scripture   Rev. W. J. Powell, Pastor
                    Old Ship A.M.E. Zion Church

Introduction of Speaker   Rev. J. C. Parker, Pastor
                    Hall Street Baptist Church

Selection by the choir*

Sermon   Dr. M. L. King, Sr., Pastor
                    Ebenezer Baptist Church, Atlanta, Ga.

Prayer of Installation   Rev. B. D. Lambert, Pastor
                    Maggie Street Baptist Church

Selection by Choir*

Charge to the Minister   Dr. M. C. Cleveland, Pastor
                    Day Street Baptist Church

Charge to the Church   Mr. T. M. Alexander, Trustee
                    Friendship Baptist Church, Atlanta, Georgia

Selection by the choir*

Welcome on Behalf of the Churches of the Community   Dr. H. H. Johnson
                    Pastor, Hutchinson Street Baptist Church

Response—Rev. M. L. King, Jr.

Offering

Benediction—Rev. M. L. King, Jr.

*The Ebenezer Baptist Church Choir, Atlanta, Georgia

 Mrs. M. L. King, Sr., Organist-Director

Table Of Contents

Preface

In July 1992, my family and I were in route to Maxwell Air Force Base, Alabama. We vacationed at my in-laws in Suffolk, Virginia, for two weeks. When in Virginia, I usually go to Richmond for a day and visit colleagues, friends, and professors. While in Richmond, I was informed by several faculty members from the School of Theology, Virginia Union University, that an alumnus, Richard W. Wills, had recently been called to be the pastor of Dexter Avenue King Memorial Baptist Church, Montgomery, Alabama.

My family and I visited Dexter on the last Sunday in August 1992. I introduced myself to Reverend Wills on that occasion. I told him a few weeks later that our rendezvous in Montgomery was no accident and God had a special work for our hands. Neither of us knew what it was at the time.

In August 1993 Dr. Wills invited me to conduct the Wednesday night Bible study at the church for six weeks. Following the traditional scripture reading and prayer period each Wednesday evening, I came forward for forty-five minutes or an hour and discussed with those in attendance my first publication, *From the Descent to the Exodus: Five Unresolved Issues*. I also shared some of my current research and its theological relevance for the Black Experience in America.

During these six weeks, senior members of the church brought up two names on several occasions. The names were Vernon Johns and Martin Luther King, Jr. I was surprised to discover that so many parishioners who knew both men were still in the church. The people shared stories with me about Reverend Johns and Reverend King. I asked had they recorded any of their recollections. The response was no. One individual informed me that a collection of King stories was attempted about fifteen or twenty years earlier.

My six-week presentation concluded. However, a restlessness came over me. Many of the persons who knew Reverend Johns and Reverend King are upwards of sixty years of age. The thought would not depart from me—What will happen with the stories about the Johns and King ministries, the latter especially, when this element is called to their eternal rest?

I approached my co-laborer in the gospel and theologue, Dr. Wills, about the possibility of compiling the recollections of Reverend King as pastor, especially since no work had been done in that area. The stories possessed by parishioners were too wonderful to remain untold. Dr. Wills presented the idea to the congregation.

Those who realized the historical and eternal value of their eyewitness accounts willingly released their memories. The literate community will be forever grateful to the small number who separated themselves, stepped forward, and gladly shared their reflections on one of the most influential personalities to live in the last five centuries. Thanks be to God for these voices that refused to remain silent.

All persons who knew Reverend King as pastor have a story that the world will never know unless they reveal it. Those who declined to share their reflections have consciously lowered themselves from the high and honorable position to which history had hoisted them. They have also denied humanity and members of their race access to facts that would have undoubtedly shed greater light on Reverend King as pastor and the movement which he guided. Indeed, one day we shall overcome, but there is much the race must first overcome. Also, those who knew Reverend King as a pastor, but remained silent, probably possess enough insights about the Montgomery Bus Boycott and the years immediately thereafter to shake modern scholarship to the foundation.

The scripture says, "Know the truth and the truth shall make you free." Those who know the story (the truth) best are obligated to document it. History provides permanent sanctuary only to those who put the eternal seal of truth on events by telling what actually transpired. Nobody can tell your story like you can.

A people who fail to record their history will restrict and limit their future, as well as that of their descendants. There is no strength, safety, or security in silence for oppressed people. They must write and preserve the details of their historical journey. At best silence will provide temporary shelter. The only certain event that will grow out of silence among the oppressed is their continued suffering. By failing to put their history in writing African Americans invite and place upon themselves and their children especially the burden of continued suffering. There is no burden so frustratingly heavy to bear as that which is borne unnecessarily and could have been easily avoided with just a little foresight. There is no suffering so fruitless, weakening, and undignified as that which is self-imposed.

There is much historical information swirling around the African-American community in Montgomery. This much became obvious during the compilation of these reflections. Readers will realize that it is impossible for persons to talk about Reverend King's ministry without providing details about the Montgomery Bus Boycott and events that followed. Some historical facts within these pages have never been shared with the reading public.

In fact, unshared historical information pertinent to the years 1954 to 1968 abounds in African-American communities across the South. Tens of thousand of African Americans participated in the movement. However, when the number of journals, diaries, and publications from the hands of those who labored for the cause are catalogued, the sum leads one to think that only a few hundred people were involved or the work was unsuccessful. Neither was the case. Thousands participated and the movement was successful.

Many senior persons within African-American communities who participated in the movement are frequently called upon to address audiences and recount their experience of thirty or forty years ago. That is all well and good. However, African Americans must sooner or later acknowledge and surrender to the power of the pen. If those who initiated and lived through one of the most unforgettable eras of American history fail to record the accomplishments for the sake of accuracy and the benefit of future generations, it is their own fault. It is unfair and unrealistic to expect observers to write the story. Those who waged the struggle must have enough pride in their accomplishments to record them.

The African-American community has approximately one quarter of a century remaining to put in writing for the world their experiences from the Civil Rights Era. This assessment appears reasonable. Twenty-five years from now adults who participated in the movement will be deceased or too old to accurately recall events. The race will have missed the opportunity to tell this story from its own perspective. All other perspectives are second rate in value.

Neither the editor nor assistant editor of this work will receive any remuneration for their efforts. Their reward is knowing that a small piece of the story has been preserved for all time. All royalties from this work will remain where they rightfully belong—with Dexter Avenue King Memorial Baptist Church and the Montgomery community.

Wally G. Vaughn
Richard W. Wills
Montgomery, Alabama
June 1995

Introduction

The public career of Martin Luther King, Jr., is divided into two distinct periods. The first period was from 1954-1960, when he was the pastor of Dexter Avenue Baptist Church, 454 Dexter Avenue, Montgomery, Alabama. This was the only church he ever served as pastor.

The second period of his public life was from January 1961-April 1968. During this latter stage, Reverend King was not the pastor of a church. His time and energy were devoted to enhancing the lives of millions of Americans and people in general. Most of the written material regarding Martin Luther King, Jr., centers around the second period of his public career.

Very little has been written about Martin Luther King, Jr., the pastor. This work is limited to the first period of his public ministry, 1954-1960. There is only a small number of individuals who can speak about Martin Luther King, Jr., as *pastor*. This group is getting smaller each year. Their contribution at this time in history is extremely crucial.

Within these pages are the reflections of individuals who were members of Dexter Avenue Baptist Church when the young Martin King was called to be the pastor. Many of those who have provided stories voted for Reverend King to fill the pulpit in 1954. He was called to be their pastor. Most still affectionately refer to him as "Reverend King." This was the first title by which they came to identify him. That identification has not been eroded. A few still refer to him as Brother Pastor. Forty years later many of them have now decided to share their recollections of Dexter's renowned pastor. Each interview recorded was conducted individually. There was no rehearsing. Each contributor will know what the others have stated upon publication. Only where there are husband and wife reflections does each know what the other shared.

Because this work is limited to a specific period and all of the contributors participated in or were eyewitnesses to many of the same events several episodes are necessarily repeated. However, each person brings his or her personal insight to the event recounted.

This publication is not a theological work and the contributors are not interested in providing a summation of Reverend King's life and work. They simply want to share some recollections of their pastor and help preserve this unusual and seldom noticed aspect of his life, labor, and calling. Second-hand accounts are usually inundated with embellishments and exaggerations. This disturbing trend is absent from these retrospective eyewitness accounts. This work has all of the elements one expects to find in a compelling story. There are within these pages scenes of humor, excitement, sadness, and surprise.

After the bus boycott started, Reverend King became a community pastor of sorts. Several reflections are provided from persons in the community between 1954 and 1960. Their accounts show the consistency of Reverend King's ministry and that his ministry expanded beyond the pulpit of Dexter Avenue Baptist Church.

This manuscript illumines the work of Reverend King from a different perspective, provides new historical insights, and will force historians to re-assess some popular assertions regarding personalities and events from 1954-1960 in Montgomery.

Deacon Robert D. Nesbitt, Sr.

In 1953 I was the clerk of the Dexter Avenue Baptist Church and Chairman of the Pulpit Committee. I was employed by Pilgrim Health Life Insurance Company as an auditor. I was auditing the Atlanta District in 1954. Atlanta was the largest district. Mr. W. C. Peden was the / manager in Atlanta.

I said to W. C. in the Atlanta office:

"Dexter is looking for a pastor."

Reverend Vernon Johns had been gone from the church for some time.

W. C. said: "Bob, I have just the man for you."

"Who is he," I inquired.

"Mike King."

"Who is Mike King?"* I asked casually. I had never heard the name.

"He is a fine young fellow. His daddy is pastor of Ebenezer Baptist Church here in Atlanta."

"Get him on the phone," I urged.

W. C. made the initial contact on a Tuesday. Martin had not yet received his doctorate degree. W. C. arranged for me to meet the young King on Friday at 2:00 p.m.

Well, on Friday I went to 200 Johnson Street. The senior King answered the door. I told the senior King who I was and why I had come to his home. I was escorted by the father to the room where the son was sitting. Martin was at the dining table eating some pork chops. Those were his favorite. I explained my mission to Martin. After I finished, I heard: "Martin, you don't want to go to that big nigger church. You are not going to be able to get along with them." The senior King caught himself, snapped his fingers, and prepared to bow out of the conversation: "Martin, I will not try to influence you. Go if you like."

I directed my attention from Martin to the senior King.

"Our church is not like that now," I commenced. "Many of the people you are concerned about have died. One woman in particular moved recently."

The father was concerned about his son. That was natural and understandable. The senior King left the dining area. Martin and I were alone. I told him that W. C. had recommended him.

"That was mighty kind of W. C.," he complimented.

---

* Rev. Martin Luther King, Jr., was called "Mike" from an early age.

I told Martin some of what he could expect at Dexter, if the church felt led to call him to be the pastor. He asked me various questions and I answered them as best I could. Four matters concerned him. Martin inquired about the size of the church. Secondly he questioned me about the membership. This was brought on by the remark made earlier by his father.

"About two-thirds of the Alabama State College faculty attends church at Dexter. There are many other professional persons in the congregation. The principal of one of the largest schools also worships at Dexter," I revealed.

Martin's third concern involved his education.

"I have not finished my Ph.D. Will the people work with me?" I told him I felt certain the Dexter family would allow him to continue his academic pursuits.

"Will they accept a man my age?"

This was the fourth matter that he desired my feedback on.

We talked a little while longer and then I prepared to leave. Martin walked with me outside. We stood on the front steps and as I got ready to walk down Martin said:

"I have been called to First Baptist Church in Chattanooga. I am supposed to be there on Sunday to give them an answer."

This revelation took me by surprise.

"Well," I began, "tell them the Lord is still speaking to you. If they are interested, First Baptist will wait for you."

He went on to First Baptist, Chattanooga, Tennessee, that Sunday. I do not know what happened or what was said.

I returned to Montgomery and made arrangements for Martin to come to Dexter and preach three Sundays later. I told the congregation about the young preacher in Atlanta and that he would be coming to preach for us. Martin was twenty-five years of age. He looked like a little boy. I knew from the beginning I was going to have to fight that issue. I told the people how old Martin was before he came to preach his first sermon.

"A boy cannot pastor this church," was the constant cry.

When Martin came three Sundays later, he preached from the subject, "Five Dimensions of Life." It was an outstanding sermon. The church fell in love with him that Lord's day. He knew quite a few of our members who were Morehouse graduates. The people would have voted him in that Sunday, if a vote had been taken.

I said to Martin after the service:

"We don't call a preacher based on the first sermon. Every minister has at least one good sermon."

Martin laughed and rejoined:

"You are right. We always put forth our best to get a job."

"You must come and preach again."

He preached a few more times. When the vote was taken, he was unanimously approved. The church officially extended the call. We met later and presented him information regarding salary and such. Martin came to Dexter on a promised salary of $5,000.00 annually. He never made a fuss over money.

He was a dynamic young pastor. Martin was outstanding in the pulpit. We left church each Sunday with a message. Even when he took his seat you would still be gasping for more. What he said and how he said it was so rich, fresh, and powerful.

During his first year, our pastor's reputation as a dynamic speaker was spreading across the city of Montgomery. His oratorical skills were evident from his first appearance at Dexter. People started coming to Dexter to hear the young minister. They were obviously talking about him around town. Gradually the crowd enlarged. This was before the movement commenced or Martin Luther King, Jr., became a household name. Martin was only in Alabama a short time before he was in demand around the state. Pastors invited him all around Alabama to preach on special occasions such as the pastor's anniversary or choir celebration.

Martin endeared himself to the Dexter membership, especially the young people. The young people loved him. Martin organized the young adults. He felt this group had much to offer the church. They were pushed by him to do more for Christ Jesus. Young people were encouraged to get involved in church activities.

About a year after Martin came to Montgomery the episode involving Mrs. Rosa Parks occurred. Mr. E. D. Nixon, a well-known community leader at the time, secured Mrs. Parks' release from jail. Several citizens gathered in the basement of Dexter after she made bail. Mr. E. D. Nixon invited the leading Black pastors in the city to Dexter for a meeting. I was not at that meeting. Martin was elected as the leader before the Montgomery Improvement Association (MIA) was formally organized. Mr. Nixon apparently had it fixed in his mind that the young pastor of Dexter was going to be the leader of the group. He had probably been observing Martin. Mr. Nixon undoubtedly felt that the time was right and the right man, Reverend King, was available. Mr. Nixon had already been laboring in the community to secure rights for Black people and his commitment to the advancement of his race was well known. However, Mr. Nixon lacked the necessary depth to sell the program to the people and gain their support. He could not have led a movement.

This observation is in no way intended to belittle Mr. Nixon or his work. He was a dynamic community man. Securing the release of Mrs.

Parks and calling the meeting, seizing the moment to initiate a protest, and helping engineer the election of Martin are evidence of his insight. Mr. Nixon knew there was no other minister in Montgomery at the time who could have risen to the occasion. Martin had not done anything spectacular since arriving which suggested he should ascend to the leadership position. However, Mr. Nixon saw something in Martin and so did many others.

To further illustrate my point about the right leader I will also lift up my former pastor Dr. Vernon Johns. He was one of the greatest orators I have ever heard. He pastored Dexter Baptist Church for four and one-half years and was Martin's predecessor. During his tenure as pastor, I never once saw Dr. Johns read from the bible. He never needed to open a bible. He knew it from cover to cover. He could quote scripture unendingly.

Reverend Johns wanted Black people in Montgomery to live fuller and richer lives. His contention was that they needed to take their destiny into their own hands. Dr. Johns managed to get some people to open a store in Mobile Heights, which was a Black section of Montgomery. With a store in their neighborhood the people would not have to travel a great distance to shop and would keep their monies in their community. The store was in business for a little over one year and then it closed. Dr. Johns had a vision and the depth needed to lead, but he was too violent. His philosophy was "I want it and I want it now."

Dr. Johns paid his money to ride the city bus one day and was instructed to go to the rear and enter. He refused and demanded his money back. The white bus driver threw the coins on the ground. In a manner that was out of character for a Black person at that time, he told the driver:

"I ought to drag you off of that bus and whip you."

Dr. Johns could not have ushered in the new era that Montgomery and the South was about to enter.

Martin accepted the leadership position and brought it to the church for approval. The church approved.

The Montgomery Improvement Association (MIA) held its first mass meeting at Holt Street Baptist Church. Martin had the complete following of the Black ministers in the city. The leading clergy presented him as our leader that night. Each pastor indicated that he was prepared to follow Martin's leadership because every minister felt the right man was in Montgomery at the right time in history.

Holt Street Baptist Church was packed that first night. People were standing outside and by the raised windows so they could hear. Martin explained what the movement was about and what we had to do to make it successful.

"We have to love one another and love those who do evil," he said.

The governor of the state had two white informants in attendance that night. Informants were at all of the mass meetings. When it was time to collect money, I used to tease them as I passed the collection plate in their direction. Informants constantly assessed the situation and reported to the proper white people. The MIA wanted three requests honored by the city. They were: more Black bus drivers hired, seating on city buses to be on a first come first served basis, and Black people be allowed to enter the bus at the front like everyone else.

The bus company turned down all three requests. It was decided that we would protest for one day. Leaflets were prepared and over the weekend circulated in the Black community. On Monday morning the buses started rolling. I only saw one Black person on a bus. Martin rode around town following the buses just to see what was happening. This one day event was so successful that another meeting was held. We decided to extend the protest, believing that we could win.

We started having mass meetings every Monday night. Often you had to get to the church early in the afternoon in order to get a seat. The larger churches in the city were used for the mass meetings. People would inquire about what night Martin was speaking. On the nights that Martin spoke one had to get to the church very early. The people loved him. When he entered to speak at the mass meetings, the people would just become emotionally lifted. They would applaud for upwards of five minutes. While walking to the microphone, Martin would shake their hands, pat them on the head, and kiss them.

After the protest had been going on for sometime, meetings were so well attended and the organization of events so refined that we had to start having the mass meetings twice a week. Monday and Thursday nights became the gathering periods.

After observing things for sometime, I think the informants basically told the governor that the people were with Martin and there was no way to curb the momentum or derail the movement. They were correct.

Monies miraculously came to the treasury of the movement. Martin was often invited to speak around the country. The Dexter congregation did not mind him going. In fact, Martin's going and coming put Dexter on the map. Audiences gave him large honorariums. Upon returning to Montgomery, he deposited his lecture earnings in the treasury to aid the movement. Supporters and speakers from other states came to Montgomery. They usually brought with them a financial contribution from churches and citizens in their communities.

The Black citizens in Montgomery were asked to stop riding the buses and join the protest. They did so willingly. After the bus boycott was well on the way, Martin informed the preachers that since the people had been asked to protest and not ride the buses they could not be left to find their own means of transportation to and from work. Martin felt that the movement was duty-bound to provide transportation for the Black workers who were protesting. He suggested to the ministers that monies from the treasury be used to help purchase station wagons. This was a wise and insightful move. Had not this creative measure been implemented there is no telling what might have happened regarding the ongoing determination of the people. Many of the churches made substantial donations toward this cause. Many of the congregations had the name of their church on the sides of station wagons.

Reverend B. J. Sims was the transportation coordinator. He did an outstanding job.

The station wagons were not the only source of transportation. Many individuals drove people around in their private automobiles. Martin appreciated the support of and relied on the Montgomery pastors who initially backed him. Young Martin was especially fond of Reverend B. D. Lambert, who was the pastor of Maggie Street Baptist Church. Lambert was some kind of preacher and Martin was crazy about him. He loved having Lambert present. Reverend Lambert was a motivator. Martin also had the highest respect for Reverend Lambert. Martin said once:

"Reverend Lambert has the finest private library of any preacher I know."

The two lived only a short distance from each other. Martin used to go to the Reverend Lambert's home and read.

Every participant in the boycott was valuable as far as Martin was concerned. There was a lady in Montgomery called the Pie Lady. She sold pies every day. Martin loved and cared for her just as much as he did for anyone else.

"The Ph.D. and the no D are all somebody in my sight," he often said.

I must admit that initially Dexter members had a let's see attitude regarding the protest movement. However, when all saw that the ministers in the city were with Martin, we threw all of our influence behind him.

The bus boycott continued. Martin remained cool, calm, and collected through it all. The success of the boycott was due to his leadership and also because of the fact that the white establishment (the city fathers) could not divide us. We were supporters of King.

The white establishment labored vigorously to undermine the movement and divide the Black community. They attempted to use other Black people on the inside, as it were, to accomplish this end. For example, the whites got to Reverend Fields. He was the secretary of the MIA. The whites paid him money to work their plan from within. Reverend Fields tried to divide us, but could not. His time was short-lived.

Reverend Fields left town and went to Africa. I do not know if he is still alive.

Reverend Fields, in a sense, had to leave Montgomery. Any Black preacher in the city, after the protest was well under way, who was opposed to Martin Luther King, Jr., in any manner was in bad shape. Black preachers who were not with Martin did not have to answer to him, but those preachers certainly had to answer smartly to their congregations.

The white establishment tried to get white families to fire Black domestic workers. It would have been almost impossible for domestic workers to secure any other employment. However, this design failed also.

The local white establishment remained disturbed. Unable to upset the movement from without or from within, legal tactics were employed.

"The Black folk mean business," the whites were saying. "We must get King."

The Internal Revenue Service paid him a visit. The state IRS contended that we were paying Martin more than the documents reflected. I had the records to show otherwise. The matter was taken to court. Most of the judges refused to hear the case. Judge Carter heard the case. After seeing our records, Judge Carter threw the case out of court.

Martin also had to withstand friction from within the movement. For example, Mr. E. D. Nixon, who basically engineered the election of Martin to head the movement, became frustrated and separated himself from the movement. Everything was going great and results were being achieved. Our aim was being accomplished. Mr. Nixon's disillusionment stemmed from feelings of being lost in the turn of events and receiving too little attention. Martin never put forth any effort to eclipse Mr. Nixon. After he was elected to head the protest, all attention, locally and nationally, naturally focused on Martin. The leader will always receive the most attention.

I was concerned for Martin's safety after the movement started. He knew I was afraid for him. Martin would be at the church until 2:00 a.m. and 3:00 a.m. working on a sermon or reading. Back then we had an underpass like a tunnel that led into the basement of the church. It would have been very easy for somebody to hide and attack him as he was leaving at night. I used to say:

"Martin, you do not need to be at the church that late."

"Brother Nesbitt, the Lord will take care of me," he would reply.

On one occasion I countered:

"Martin, God has given you good sense and wants you to use it."

He concurred and said, regarding his late stays at the church: "You are right. I will do better."

Martin was fortunate not to have been assassinated in Montgomery. Of course, Dexter is located in the heart of town and near the capitol. I think the location partially protected him.

Martin remained calm under the most frightening circumstances. We were in a mass meeting at First Baptist Church one night. I was in the pulpit. It was my task to ask for monies. After Mr. Nixon resigned, Martin appointed me the treasurer of the movement. I noticed constant moving on the far end of the pulpit area. I knew something had happened. I just did not know what. The whispering and moving continued. I learned that the parsonage had been bombed. The ministers on the pulpit agreed unanimously that this news could not be shared immediately with the people seated in the congregation. There was no telling what the people would have done.

Martin was slipped out of the side door. When he arrived at the parsonage, a large angry mob of supporters were standing in the front yard. Martin waved his way through the crowd, rushed in, and found his wife Coretta, their only child at the time, and Mrs. Lucy Williams safe. The latter usually sat with Coretta when Martin had to speak at the mass meetings. After consoling those in the house, he went and stood on the front porch. Martin raised his hands, got the people's attention, and his voice rang out in the dark.

"My wife is fine and so is the baby. Mrs. Lucy Williams is fine. We are still non-violent. I want you to go home and put away your weapons," Martin said.

The people were angry and ready to erupt, but they listened and obeyed. Their leader had spoken.

There were certain white people in Montgomery who knew what Martin was saying and doing was right. However, there was another element that felt differently and was out to destroy him at any cost. The bombing of the parsonage was not intended to kill anyone. Those who planted the device knew that Martin was not at home. The bomb could have been designed and packed with far more power. The bombing was comparable to a warning shot being fired in the air. Opponents wanted to get Martin's attention, rattle him, and try to force the young preacher to re-think his position.

Martin would not turn around. He was fearless and determined to cling to his convictions. He had a philosophy and belief that could not be altered regardless of the circumstance. Martin felt the role he was filling was his God-appointed destiny.

Following this incident some of the men of the church offered Martin and his family round-the-clock protection. We took it into our own hands. Men sat inside the King home by a window each night. There was only one individual with whom Martin had a problem. We had a member of the church who had retired from the United States Army. He had his assigned nights to guard the pastor's home. Martin found out that the retired soldier kept a gun on his person. Martin called the church officers together and explained:

"I do not need that. I must live what I preach. I preach non-violence."

We got the message. The services of this one gentleman were discontinued.

There was a member of the church named Winston Craig. He was a chauffeur for the governor. Brother Craig also drove Martin to several places for speaking engagements. I made several of these trips with Brother Craig and the pastor. Martin would write his sermon or speech out, leave it in the car, and go address the audience. He was never bound to a manuscript. This freedom always provided for a richer livelier speech by Martin.

In May 1957 Martin gave the keynote address in front of the Lincoln Memorial during the Prayer Pilgrimage for Freedom. The speech was entitled, "Give Us the Ballot—We Will Transform the South." Martin's attorney, Mr. Fred Gray, and I went to Washington also. Mr. Gray and I were seated right down front. Martin did an excellent job with that address. This was the public address that ignited his ascent to national prominence.

Following the speech and the conclusion of the event, I greeted Martin and said:

"Brother Pastor, that was a good speech. You did a very fine job, but you read the whole thing."

This was not a critical observation. Martin never read his speeches and addresses and there was a glaring difference on this occasion to those of us who knew him and his oratorical style. Perhaps Martin read his speech on this occasion because it was delivered in the nation's capital and people all across the United States would hear it.

Pleased with the compliment yet surprised by my observation the pastor asked:

"How could you tell?" Before I could answer he added: "You are correct. I read the speech. I read all of it."

Martin loved children and had a special sympathy for boys and girls from depressed communities. There were several YMCA facilities in Montgomery. However, one was needed in the Black community for the youth who resided in a particular depressed neighborhood. Martin was moved by this need. The YMCA agreed to give a specified amount to this particular facility, but the community had to make up the difference. The Black parents on that side of town were poor and could not have come up with the requested sum. Martin suggested that they donate the needed $20,000.00 from the organization's purse for the sake of the children. His wish was granted.

One Sunday after the worship service I was downstairs with some of the other church officers. The Sunday offering was being counted. On his way from the pastor's study, Martin said:

"Brother Nesbitt, come by my house after you are done here."

I knew at that very moment Martin was getting ready to leave Dexter and Montgomery. The Lord revealed that to me the moment Martin asked me to come by the parsonage.

After everything was done at the church, I drove over to Jackson Street. I got out of my car, walked up to the door, and rang the bell. Martin opened the door. I was about to enter the house, when he said:

"Let's talk on the porch."

"Alright."

"Brother Nesbitt, I am going to resign from Dexter."

"Oh, no," I said. I was not completely surprised, but I was deeply moved.

"You are the first to know," Martin revealed. "You recommended me to the church. You were the first person I met from the congregation. You brought me here. I feel it is only right that I tell you first. I have not even told Coretta." I stood listening. The explanation was not long in coming: "Pressure is being put on the teachers and professional people in the congregation. They are having to take abuses that they could avoid, if I were out of the picture."

I said:

"I don't like it; it is your decision to leave, but I can understand what you are saying."

That was Martin. He was more concerned about the people than he was about himself.

"You know I am being called away frequently," he added. "Being gone so much is not fair to the church."

It was his position that the people needed a pastor who could shepherd them in the proper manner. Martin's greater concern was probably the first part of his reason for deciding to leave. Many in the congregation had already said they could live with him preaching at Dexter once a month. He was aware of their willingness to make such an unusual concession. While his pastoral concerns were legitimate, Martin's first explanation undergirded his decision to leave.

Martin had a 1954 Pontiac. He left Dexter Avenue Baptist Church in 1960. Martin departed Montgomery driving the same 1954 blue Pontiac. He could have departed Montgomery driving any model or make of car desired. But the way he left was the Martin Luther King, Jr., we knew as our pastor. He did not care much for material things, but cared about people.

Martin did not have any other church in mind to pastor. He left for the reasons stated. Before leaving he passed on several encouraging thoughts to the members and supporters of the MIA. First, Martin told the leaders and the followers that they must continue to love one another. That had been one of his themes throughout the movement. Secondly, he said that provisions should be made so that whatever happened we would be able to immediately come to the aid of individuals.

Martin felt he was leaving the MIA in good hands with his first lieutenant Reverend Ralph David Abernathy. Ralph kept the movement going.

Martin had great insight. He saw that a movement within the land was gaining momentum. Few others saw it. Martin became part of the Southern Christian Leadership Conference (SCLC). This organization served his purpose better and allowed him greater freedom to do what he felt led to. The organization had to take the brunt of opposition and threats rather than a church congregation made up of local citizens who could be targeted by the establishment.

It was only a short time after leaving Montgomery that Martin summoned Ralph to come to Atlanta and work with SCLC. Martin felt he could use Ralph better in that organization. Martin was a key figure in helping secure a church for Ralph in Atlanta.

The late Reverend S. S. Seay, Sr., became the leader of the MIA. He was very effective and the people followed him. Several other pastors stood at the helm of the MIA and rendered valuable service. It was an organization we all felt was so outstanding in formulating and securing civil rights for Black people in the local community. All who belonged to it felt that the MIA should continue to be a voice in determining the direction in which the local Black community should move.

The MIA continued to pursue the same goals and function under the same principles it did under Martin's leadership. We remained non-violent. All of us wanted people across the land to understand that this was a movement and organization that Martin and the people felt had the blessings of God.

It was a blessing to have had Martin Luther King, Jr., in our community.

Mr. Rufus Lewis

It has always been my contention that a people must work within the system in order to achieve their goals. I always felt strongly that Black people should have the right to vote. I took it upon myself to work for this cause and dedicated my life to it. My labors in this area commenced years before the bus boycott or the protest movement commenced. I used to go around to the homes of adults and business establishments owned by Black people and encourage them to go to the courthouse and register to vote.

It was always easier said than done. White people did not want Black people to register to vote. During the time when my personal campaign was in full swing to get members of my race registered, persons wanting to register had to take a written test at the courthouse. Many of the Black people whom I took to the registrar's office were denied the right to register because they failed the test. They did not fail because of any inability to read, write, and comprehend. A good many were literate persons. There were many professional Black people who were denied the right to register. Those in power would fail the test-taker under any pretense so as to block the individual from registering. If I took a Black person to take the test and the individual was told he failed, I would offer words of encouragement:

"Don't be discouraged. We will come back again."

I continued to take Black people to the courthouse to register one, two and three at a time. I always remained with each person while he or she took the test. I remained present to make sure Black people were not bullied by the white people. There were actually occasions when we arrived at the courthouse, the person I had escorted saw those white folk, became fearful and turned around. Many Black people simply would not have gone to the courthouse to register—which was comparable to bucking the system—had I not gone with them and stayed by their sides. I had been to the courthouse so much, having taken so many people to register, that those in charge knew me. I would not and could not rest seeing things as they were. I traveled all across Alabama, Mississippi, and Georgia trying to help and encourage Black people to register.

Even at this early date there were white politicians who approved of what I was doing. They knew of my zeal to get Black people registered. A politician wants votes. That is what will get him or her elected. They do not care much about the color of the hand that pulls the lever or marks a block.

The poll tax was no longer being used as a means of denying Black people the right to vote. The written test was now the political ploy to keep Black people out of the process. Without question there were Black adults in Montgomery who could not read and write, but there were numerous white people who could not read and write. Many in the latter class were allowed to pass the test and some were given answers.

I felt I had to come up with a creative measure to aid my people. Based on past actions Black people were going to keep going to the courthouse to take the test and be told—"You did not pass." I managed to get hold of a test. That was well over forty years ago and I do not rightly recall how the test came into my possession. I took it home. I secured a mimeograph machine and ran the test off. Initially two hundred or three hundred were run off. There were some twenty or twenty-five questions on the test.

Myself and one or two others got Black people together. Sometimes in a home or in some other setting. They were given the test to take on the spot. Questions they did not understand I explained. We coached the people on what to say and how to answer the questions. Those who passed the pre-test of sorts in this private and secret setting were scheduled by me to go to the courthouse and take the real test and register.

White politicians back then were afraid to publicly accept the Black vote or come out for Black people, but would accept a ballot if it was cast for them.

A white man who was running for office came to me and asked for support. I never made any decision alone. White candidates who courted the support of Black voters had to go before a screening committee comprised of members of the race whose vote was desired. Following an interview with the white candidate, a group determined which white candidate would get our endorsement. It was a group decision.

As mentioned earlier, I had a mimeograph machine. I would print up the ballot. People could take the ballot into the booth with them already marked. One could not use the marked ballot, but had to re-mark an authentic ballot during the actual voting process. The marked ballot, however, served as a guide. I would mark off the candidates for whom the Black people should vote. I was not a leader, nor was I telling the people who to vote for, but I encouraged them to vote for individuals who had the interest and concern of Black people at heart.

The marked or prototype ballot immensely aided those whose literacy rate was low. All this element had to do was follow the pattern, transfer to the real ballot what I had identified for them on the marked ballot. The marked ballot procedure was legal. I was not abusing or manipulating the political process. To have done something illegal would have jeopardized all of my life's work.

Around 1953 I opened a night club which was called The Citizens Club. It was located on the corner of Myles and Charlotte Streets. The

Citizens Club was the best night spot in town. Many of the older Black people in Montgomery still have fond memories of The Citizens Club. A person could not get inside unless he or she was a registered voter. That was why it was named The Citizens Club. My contention has always been that only those persons who are registered are citizens. Each person had to show a voter registration identification card before gaining entry into The Citizen's Club. Word of mouth that one was registered was not good enough. If a person confessed that he or she was not registered, I took the individual's name, address, and telephone number then turned the person away. Only a few days would elapse before I contacted them and began to make arrangements for them to be registered.

Many Black people in Montgomery had been laboring to improve the condition of the race. Meetings were being held locally and groups attempted to redress the treatment of Black people. I worked viciously to get people registered to vote. That was my project and contribution to the struggle. I basically worked alone in this endeavor. Mr. E. D. Nixon was also a serious-minded community worker.

I was a member of Dexter Avenue Baptist Church when Dr. Johns was the pastor. He and I were very good friends.

Reverend King came to pastor our church in the mid-fifties. He was an excellent speaker. He had only been pastor of Dexter Avenue Baptist Church for a short time before Mrs. Rosa Parks was arrested. Mr. E. D. Nixon rallied the ministers and some of the leading Black citizens. A meeting was held at which fifteen persons or so were present. At that time I nominated Reverend King to be the leader of the organization which later became known as the Montgomery Improvement Association. I nominated Reverend King because I was associated with him and knew him well. He was encouraged by my voter registration efforts. Though a newcomer to town, Reverend King was the best man to step up to the helm. He had the ability to reason, think matters through, and articulate. This was the top man as far as I was concerned. To accomplish anything worthwhile the best man has to be out front.

Mr. Nixon did not initially want Reverend King. The former wanted to be the leader. Nixon was ambitious, but he did not have the force or background necessary to command a large following. He had no higher education and lacked the ability to think in broad terms. This is not a criticism, but the reality of events. I told Nixon we needed someone else. We had worked together in the past and were laboring for the same just cause. I had no problem saying what I did to him. Nixon became irritated with me; however, he yielded. I was not rejecting Nixon. I was being practical. He had it in his mind that he was going to do what Reverend King ultimately accomplished. However, Nixon could not have done it. If the choices were Nixon and King, everybody knew the superior man. Nixon and I remained friends.

It was decided to have a meeting at Holt Street Baptist Church. The Black community at large was invited. I helped make up the flyers that were circulated announcing the meeting. The boycott commenced and the rest in now history.

After the boycott was underway, transportation was needed to get people to and from work. There was especially a concern about the Black women who were domestics in the homes of white families. Numerous creative methods were devised to get people to and from their places of employment.

My wife and I were transportation coordinators also. One gathering point for riders was the corner of Lawrence and Monroe Streets. If the people just got there, a ride to work was provided.

Our family owned a funeral home in Montgomery. The funeral home had several cars which were used for the grieving family on the day of a funeral. As many of these cars as possible were used in the mornings and evenings to transport people back and forth to and from work.

Reverend King only lived about a five- or ten-minute walk from my house. He would stop by frequently when walking through the neighborhood. We had several meetings and planning sessions here.

Following the conclusion of the movement Montgomery bus boycott and Reverend King's departure from Montgomery, I became an elected state legislator. I am sure that my work in the area of voter registration stood out in the minds of the electorate.

During my freshman term, President Jimmy Carter appointed me to a federal post. I was the first Black United States federal marshal in the State of Alabama.

Deacon Zelia Evans

I came to Alabama State College to teach and joined Dexter Avenue Baptist Church after arriving in Montgomery. The first time I heard Reverend King speak I said to myself after the message, "My, my, what a speaker."

He was called to be our pastor. The first new idea Reverend King presented to the Dexter Avenue Baptist Church congregation was the Month Clubs. The Month Clubs idea was a part of his 1954-55 fiscal year recommendation to the church. He explained the idea and read his recommendation to us as follows:

> In order that every member of the church shall be identified with a smaller and more intimate fellowship of the church, clubs representing the twelve months of the year shall be organized. Each member of the church will automatically become a member of the club of the month in which he or she was born. Those born in January will be members of the *"January"* Club. Those born in February will be members of the *"February"* Club, etc. Each month club shall choose its own officers. Each club shall meet once per month, with the exception of the month for which the club is named. In the month for which the club is named, each club shall meet weekly. So the December Club, for example, shall meet once monthly until December. In December it shall meet each week. Each club shall be asked to make a special contribution to the church on the last Sunday of the month for which it is named. Also, on the Church Anniversary each club shall be asked to contribute at least one hundred dollars ($100.00). All of the money raised by these clubs shall be placed in a fund known as the building fund. The work of these clubs shall be to supplement that of the Building Fund Committee. (This committee will be discussed subsequently).

The Month Clubs are still active groups at Dexter Avenue King Memorial Baptist Church. Other churches have also organized month clubs.

Reverend King was involved in all phases of church activities. I recall presiding at a June club meeting which the pastor attended. It was held at the residence of Mrs. Susie J. Govan on Hutchinson Street. Reverend King was an active participant. He shared in the discussions of agenda items, enjoyed the delicious repast and engaged in informal discussions. Later that evening the June Club members played a game of musical chairs. Reverend King, like everyone else, was racing around seeking a chair before the music stopped. His presence and participation brought delight to the meeting.

Reverend King was an excellent leader with gifted abilities. He had the ability to organize the membership for action.

He took the greatest pastoral interest in the Dexter flock. This interest continued even after Reverend King's fame began to spread. A consoling visit to my hospital room by Reverend King was very inspiring. He was scheduled to speak out of town. On his way to Dannelly Field the pastor stopped by Saint Jude Hospital. I was impressed yet concerned about his seeming non-recognition of the time especially since he had a scheduled flight.

"You need to go on to the airport," I said. "You cannot miss your flight. There are people waiting to hear what you have to say.'

"I won't miss my flight. I had to stop by and see you."

We talked a little longer. Reverend King prayed with and for me then departed.

A highlight of Reverend King's pastorate was the annual church conference which was held at the beginning of the church year. During the conference there were dinner meetings, with the Women's Council serving as hosts. We would consume a delicious meal, engage in a game, and then attend to agenda items. The main agenda item was the pastor's message. His powerful presentation reviewed the previous year's activities and accomplishments, after which he enumerated recommendations for the coming year and challenged us to move forward. In his presentation, Reverend King would begin by commending the congregation for the accomplishments of the past year. He would then address the *hows* and *whys* of his recommendations. In his challenge, he urged us always to turn our missions courageously toward the future.

"This," he said on one occasion, "is our profound challenge and our overwhelming responsibility."

In these meetings Reverend King exhibited true leadership.

During Reverend King's pastorate, the church received an invitation to his sister Christine's wedding. In commenting about it to the church congregation Reverend King declared that his usual analytical and comprehensive interview would be held by him with the couple in view of its role pertinent to this important event affecting their lives. His sister, he said, would not be excluded.

The church decided to send Elizabeth M. Arrington and Zelia S. Evans as official attendants for the ceremony. They were weekend guests of Pastor and Mrs. King. Joining them for the ceremony and reception were Trustee Chairperson and Mrs. C. T. Smiley, Deacon and Mrs. Robert D. Nesbitt, Sr., Trustee and Mrs. Franklyn W. Taylor, Sr., Billy Taylor, Mrs. Catherine Maddox Osborne, Deacon and Mrs. Richmond P. Smiley, Mrs. Eleanor Sippial, Mrs. Gussie Carter and Mrs. Mamie Griffin. Rev. & Mrs.

King hosted the Dexter group for lunch at Paschal's Hotel after the gala events.

I worked at Alabama State College. One year an enlarged enrollment required that we extend the registration dates. We had to work on a Sunday morning. Our duties were completed just in time for me to attend church. I rushed out to Jackson Street hoping to catch a ride to church. Fortunately a car passed in which Reverend King was riding. A driver was taking him to church. Reverend King had the driver stop and pick me up.

I got in the back seat. Reverend King was in the front. After greeting me he looked back and said:

"I'm writing my sermon for the morning."

Later, when the church bulletin called for the sermon, Reverend King approached the pulpit without a manuscript. True to form, this sermon was characterized by length, breadth and depth. As usual, it was delivered without a manuscript.

Reverend King never passed anyone without greeting them. One day, while walking across Dexter Avenue and Commerce Street, I glimpsed the wave of a hand during the busy rush hour. I took a second glance and discovered it was Reverend King employing the gesture and a smile to get my attention and speak to me.

Reverend King frequently expressed regrets that his presidency of the Montgomery Improvement Association and his involvement in Civil Rights activities consumed time that he desired to use to fulfill pastoral obligations. The members assured him that they supported him and were willing to assist him in view of the urgency of the demands on his time and his leadership.

Reverend King maintained exact records. He believed that the history of the church and activities of the congregation should be recorded. Below is his pastoral report of activities for 1954-55, 1955-1956 and 1956-1957:

Pastoral Activities 1954-55

Sermons preached at Dexter	46
Sermons preached at other churches	7
Sermons and lectures at Colleges	13
Community and Civic Meetings attended	36
Pastoral visits	87
Sick visits	49
Baptized	12
Marriages performed	5
Funerals preached	5
Children dedicated	2
Personal Interviews and Conferences	22
Books read	26
Periodicals read	102
Represented the Church in District,	

State & National Conventions	10
Doctoral Dissertation completed	

Pastoral Activities 1955-56

Sermons preached at Dexter	36
Sermons preached at other churches	16
Sermons and lectures at Colleges	8
Community and Civic Meetings attended	110
Pastoral visits	42
Sick visits	38
Baptized	6
Marriages performed	5
Funerals preached	3
Children dedicated	2
Personal Interviews and Conferences	20
Books read	21
Periodicals read	96
Represented the Church in District	
State & National Convention	9

Pastoral Activities 1956-57

Sermons preached at Dexter	30
Sermons and lectures away from home	50
Community and Civic Meetings attended	115
Pastoral visits	24
Sick visits	20
Baptized	9
Marriages performed	4
Funerals preached	2
Children dedicated	3
Personal Interviews and Conferences	45
Books read	10
Periodicals read	85
Represented the Church in District,	
State & National Conventions	10

Community demands on Reverend King increased. He became concerned about the spiritual growth and development of Dexter Avenue Baptist Church. An outgrowth of his feelings and concerns led him to make the following recommendation in his annual address presented to the church conference on the evening of October 23, 1957, which included a report of activities for 1956-57 and recommendations for 1957-58. The recommendation was as follows:

A Coordinating Council shall be appointed to assist the pastor in coordinating the work of the various auxiliaries and organizations of the church. This council will check with the various organizations of the church from time to time to see if they are moving on with their program. In other words, the main work of this council will be to assist the pastor in implementing the program of the church. It will seek to give new blood to those organizations that have become stagnant. The council should meet at least once every two months to discuss ways to improve the general program of the church. The council shall consist of the following persons: Dr. Zelia S. Evans, Chairman; Mr. J. H. Gilchrist, Co-Chairman; Miss Verdie Davie, Dr. J. T. Brooks, Mr. T. H. Randall, Mrs. Thelma Anderson, Mrs. E. M. Arrington.

An interesting incident occurred during the presentation of Reverend King's report of activities for 1956-57 and recommendations for 1957-58. The church conference was always held in the lower level of the church. The telephone rang in the office adjacent to where we were assembled. A young lady answered it and exhibited inquisitive expressions as she stood in the door upon her return. Reverend King acknowledged her presence.

The young lady said: "Dr. Pettus says it's a boy."

Applause and expressions of joy erupted.

When partial quietness was restored, Deacon C. J. Dunn inquired:

"What are you going to name him?"

In exuberant and emphatic words, Reverend King replied:

"Martin Luther King, III."

The meeting continued and was dismissed on time. As usual, the meeting was prolonged informally by conversations with individuals after dismissal.

There was expressed anxiety by some of us to Reverend King that these conversations be deferred in order that he might reach the hospital and see his newborn son and wife before closing hour at the hospital. Mrs. Leola H. Whitted's concern prompted her to telephone the hospital, express our concern, and ask that our pastor be admitted upon arrival. Mrs. Whitted was assured that Reverend King would be allowed to spend time with his wife and son.

The annual church conference for the year 1958 went as in previous years. Below are the pastor's introductory expressions. They will give readers a feel for how our church conferences were conducted. Reverend King read as follows on 8 November 1958:

> We stand again on the threshold of a new church year. As we prepare to enter this new church year, we may gain guidance and direction by reviewing the experiences of the past.
>
> The 1957-58 church year was another year of spiritual advance. While we lost several good members through death and the process of moving to other sections of the country, we have continued to move on, replacing these persons whenever we could. So in spite of these losses our membership remains about the same. The new members who have joined

our fellowship this year have, by and large, given themselves unreservedly to the program of the church.

Financially, we have again demonstrated spiritual maturity. Members have given with a real consciousness of Christian stewardship. Receipts from all sources have exceeded twenty-two thousand dollars ($22,000.00). Of this amount we have given generously for benevolent purposes, missions, and education.

This church year witnessed the construction of a new study for the pastor in the first unit of the church. This undertaking, which cost more than three thousand dollars ($3,000.00), was ably backed by the entire church. When the job was finished the money was all paid. Two members of our official board—Julius Alexander and Winfred Meadows—did the major portion of the work. Several women of the Women's Council chose the furniture and served as interior decorators. Everyone who has seen the study admits that it is a beautiful sight to behold.

Many other significant things have taken place in the life of our church this year. Mention can only be made of a few. The "special days" throughout the church year proved to be tremendously successful. Through these occasions we were privileged to have our pulpit graced by some of the outstanding personalities of America. Each of these great speakers brought something to our community which will have a lasting effect for good.

The various auxiliaries of the church have continued to move on with great positive growth. The new Matrons Circle of the Missionary Society—bearing the name Essie M. Jette Circle—has had a phenomenal growth. It has developed into one of the strongest units of the church. We commend the chairman, Mrs. Catherine Maddox, and all of the fine young ladies working with her.

At the beginning of the church year I recommended that a coordinating council be appointed to assist the pastor in implementing the program of the church. The work of this council—headed by Dr. Zelia Evans and Mr. J. H. Gilchrist—has exceeded all expectations. Especially noteworthy is the way this council has coordinated the work of the month clubs. Every member of Dexter owes a real debt of gratitude to the members of this council.

The various committees of the church are still active and the official board still works as a unit. All of this is indicative of the fact that Dexter is still alive with full blooded activity rather than anemic passivity.

Certainly, I cannot close this message without a personal word of gratitude. As you know, this has been a rather difficult year for me. I have had to confront the brutality of police officers, and unwarranted arrest, and a near fatal stab wound by a mentally deranged woman. These things have poured upon me like staggering torrents on a cold wintry day. But throughout these ordeals, my family and I felt your prayers, concern, and moral support. I am sure that your thoughtful, considerate gestures of goodwill gave me the courage and strength to face the ordeals of that trying period. For three long months I found it impossible to occupy the pulpit. But you carried on in my absence in a high and noble manner. For all of this, I am thankful beyond the power of words to express.

In closing, let me say that the future is filled with vast possibilities—the future of our church and the future of the community. It is my hope that we will move into this promising future with firm commitment and deep dedication. Let us remove from our souls the shackles of fear and the manacles of despair, and move on into this uncertain but promising future with the faith that the dawn of a new day is just around the horizon.

Reverend King's report of pastoral activities for the year 1957-58 are recorded below:

Pastoral Chores

Sermons preached at Dexter	28
Sermons and lectures away from home	54
Community and Civic meetings attended	106
Pastoral visits	20
Sick visits	26
Baptized	15
Marriages performed	6
Funerals preached	5
Children dedicated	3
Personal interviews	36
Books read	8
Periodicals read	92
Represented Church in District, State & National Conventions	9

Of course, it is obvious from the 1957-58 statistics that Reverend King delivered more sermons and lectures away from Dexter than at the church. He was in great demand.

Reverend King was a product of the Black Experience. Black religious traditions symbolized by him were: empathy with his flock, spiritual fervor, and strong leadership.

Mrs. Thelma Austin Rice

African-Americans in Montgomery were not as soft and idle in the late 1940s and early 1950s as the public has been led to believe. Years before the bus boycott numerous organizations composed of and headed by African Americans were working to secure civil rights for the race locally. There was the Emaenon Club, The Women's Political Council, Montgomery Democratic Club and others. The latter was engaged in voter registration in the late 40s and early 50s. Mr. Rufus Lewis was the MDC's most prominent member. Many other groups were involved in voter registration and civic concerns that affected the African-American community. One or two groups started out as social organizations, but as events transpired these groups became more political minded. Local civic concerns attracted them. There were a host of other organizations, such as the Federated Colored Women's Club, Men's Business League, Elks, NAACP, and National Council of Negro Women.

All of the groups did good work. Practically every organization had solid ideas. The difficulty was that none had enough clout to make events happen or the white establishment respond. No group in Montgomery before 1954/55 had the leadership that could have galvanized a movement. I knew all of the heads of the various organizations. They were bright, most of them educated, insightful, and committed. However, they all lacked the depth and force required to shake a system to its foundation.

We elected our new pastor for Dexter Avenue Baptist Church. His name was Martin Luther King, Jr. He was not elected based on any political accomplishments. Reverend King was first and foremost a minister of the gospel of our Lord. We called him to be our pastor.

I can easily summarize his preaching style. He was always eloquent. He spoke in long sentences, esoteric. His preaching moved you in a direction one way or the other. Every sermon had an element of hope. One could not help but believe there was a God. Reverend King made you believe there was a God who would hear your call.

His sermon titles were very provocative. He always left the listener thinking. Dr. King would challenge his hearers each Sunday. It was as though he intentionally wanted to shake us up. His sermons were practical and philosophical.

He was didactic in his presentation. In every sermon I heard, it seemed as if our pastor was able to bring two seemingly irreconcilable ideas or positions together. He was aware of good and evil and wrestled with them. He would keep you spellbound. Everyone might not have understood all the words and terms he used, but the way he said it and the practical application he pointed out held listeners' attention.

Pastor King's preaching had a freshness. With most ministers you did not have to follow them attentively because their words and phrases were well known. Much of what they said was like an old shoe. Reverend King's sermons were fresh and different. You were always challenged to be the person God created you to be. The God Reverend King preached about was a loving and forgiving God. This God respected the worth in all that was created. Other ministers merely preached. "If you do this or that, or fail to do this or that, you are going to hell." They preached an all-powerful God, but that God did not seem to be loving. Forgiveness was thematic in Pastor King's preaching.

Our pastor realized there was a power, greater than human strength, that would guide you. He believed God would see him through, and preached that this same God was accessible to all persons.

Dr. King had an assuredness about what he believed. It was so strong until it might have come through with a tinge of arrogance. I do not mean this in a negative manner. He had convictions and nothing could sway him.

At church or club meetings Dr. King was jovial and full of life. He was the same way at our tea gatherings. He had a grand sense of humor. In spite of his humor, there was always an immovable dignity.

The young preacher was a compassionate pastor. He would always hear you out regardless. Dr. King was never too busy to talk with another person. He had a great respect for older people.

He was an innovative open-minded pastor. He started a lecture series, which was an annual event. Well-known African-American preachers and great minds that dealt with the relevant issues of the day were invited to come and lecture. A series usually lasted three or four days and was held in the evening. The first lecturer to come was J. Pius Boubour. Several females came to address us also on special days and observances. That was a very creative step on the part of Reverend King. Few Baptist preachers in the 1950s allowed women the freedom to speak in a church from the pulpit.

Our pastor was open to new ideas for the church. He started a Young Men's Club in the Church. I do not know much about it. One of the men who belonged to it would have to provide information.

Reverend King started the birth month clubs. He appointed me president of the January Club. He was born in January and belonged to our club. The primary purpose of the birth month club was to foster fellowship that was to become contagious. The January Club held a birthday party on a designated day in January of each year in a home. Reverend King attended whenever possible. Forty years later I still have my roster with the names, birthdays, addresses and telephone numbers for the January Club. Many persons have relocated or are deceased. Their names and birthdays, however, are listed:

Alexander, Mr. J. J.	(18)	Idlett, Mrs. Willie	—
Alexander, Mr. J. T.	(27)	Jackson, Miss Alice	(22)
Alexander, Mr. W. E.	(25)	James, Miss Alice	(22)
Anderson, Miss Laurel	(31)	King, Rev. M. L.	(15)
Atkins, Mrs. Martha	(25)	Malden, Mrs. Jean	(11)
Beverly, Mrs. Margaret	(28)	Malden, Mr. Spurgeon	(09)
Bibb, Mrs. Lillian	(28)	Moore, Miss Marguerite	(21)
Blackmon, Mrs. Addrean	(18)	Nesbitt, Mr. Joe, Sr.	(15)
Brannon, Mrs. Jimmie	(5)	Nesbitt, Mr. Walter	(09)
Bryant, Mrs. Betsy	(17)	Posey, Mrs. Dorothy	(02)
Carlton, Mr. A. G.	(12)	Rice, Mrs. Thelma	(24)
Crapps, Mr. Walter	(13)	Rogers, Mrs. LaPelza	—
DeCosta, Mrs. Beautine	(30)	Sankey, Miss Myrtle	(18)
Edmondson, Mrs. Mable	(09)	Shannon, Mr. Claude	(06)
Frost, Mrs. Lizzie	(25)	Shannon, Mrs. Maggie	(26)
Gilbert, Mr. Curtis	(25)	Shannon, Miss Mary	(15)
Gilchrist, Mr. J. H.	(12)	Sheppard, Mr. W. J.	(01)
Gray, Mrs. Ruby Thorn	(31)	Vandiver, Mrs. Flossie	(06)
Hunter, Mrs. Lillie	(18)	Woods, Mr. Edward T.	(01)

These nearly forty persons gathered in different homes at designated times for fellowship, discussion, and planning. It became apparent what Reverend King's aim was and it worked. Month Club participants came together other than just on Sunday. They assembled in homes. Under ordinary circumstance we probably would not have been in each other's homes as often.

The pastor loved great music. Ebenezer Baptist Church Choir, Atlanta, Georgia, came to Montgomery one Sunday to give a concert. Daddy King was the pastor at Ebenezer. The young King could sing also. He had a beautiful voice.

The Holy Communion Services conducted by Reverend King were extremely moving. The Lord's Supper was held the first Sunday in the month in the late evening. In the South, supper is the late meal and the Lord's Supper was served in the evening. Parishioners had to return to church. At a certain point Reverend King said: "And He sat down with the twelve...." The lights were turned out and only the glow of the candles was visible. Twelve of the deacons were around Reverend King.

Holy Communion was conducted in this manner until Reverend King's schedule became very demanding. Afterward other ministers would come preach and serve communion as the occasion dictated. However, guest preachers did it differently.

Reverend King was full of energy. I recall one first Sunday in the month we had an afternoon "Tea Time" sponsored by the January and December Clubs. When the special afternoon event ended, we began to exit. It had been a long day with morning worship and the afternoon activity. I remember the pastor pointing at me, smiling, and saying:

"See you tonight. See you tonight."

He meant my presence was expected at the evening worship service which was to start in a couple of hours.

Reverend King did not favor fundraisers, though the church did have a few. He did not believe in running the church off of monies raised. His belief was that Christians should give or tithe. He preferred that members pledge or simply give to the cause of Christ.

On the evening the first mass meeting was held at Holt Street Baptist Church thousands of people were present. I stood outside with numerous others. We could not gain entry into the church. People who could not get inside were milling around outside. Everybody was uptight. There were still no definite plans regarding many issues. Mr. E. D. Nixon urged the ministers that night to rise up and face the situation. He demanded that we not take it any more. Mr. Nixon basically said—the time was right.

In retrospect, all are now convinced that the time was right and the right man, Martin Luther King, Jr., was in the right place. There was an anxiousness among the people at Holt Street Baptist Church that night. However, I was not worried about events getting out of control. Reverend King was a master *par excellence* at crowd control.

The bus boycott was basically Mr. E. D. Nixon's idea. He made such a claim on several occasions and I believe it. Mr. Nixon had the wherewithal, the tenacity, and commitment needed to make things happen, but lacked the ability to communicate with all people and groups. He had the necessary raw skills. Reverend King brought the refined dimension required.

Mr. Nixon had good insights. He was a Pullman Porter and worked with A. Philip Randolph. Mr. Nixon was exposed to the labor world and understood the power of a collective effort. He pointed out that upwards of seventy percent of the persons who rode the Montgomery buses were members of his race. He said that the Black community literally owned the buses because they were the patrons. The only thing needed was an individual to pull it off. It took someone like Mr. Nixon to see that.

Reverend King was the right man to head the protest because he brought something special to the event. That something was a part of him. A preacher always brings an ingredient to bear that no one else from any other vocation can bring. Reverend King brought that special ingredient.

He had convictions and knew what he believed. You could not shake his belief. He would not allow people to do that.

There was a large crowd that night at Holt Street Baptist Church, and large crowds at mass meetings all the nights thereafter. However, it was not the size of the crowds that sustained Reverend King. His actions would have been the same with or without a crowd.

When mass meetings were held, the people waited patiently for Dr. King to speak. His oratorical style and preaching enlisted every audience's attention. The church where a mass meeting was being held would be filled to capacity when Reverend King was scheduled to speak. When Pastor King stood up to address the body, people could be heard whispering:

"Let's listen to what God's man has to say."

If the crowd saw him approaching the pulpit, the words "Here he comes" rushed around the church.

In the Black church, the pastor and his family are special. The congregation adored the King children, Yolanda and Martin III. Mrs. King sang in the choir. When the King's first child, Yolanda, was born, Mrs. Cleonia Taylor used to hold the baby during Sunday worship service so the mother could sing. Cleonia was an usher. I can see her in my mind now seated on the back pew holding Yolanda.

After the parsonage was bombed, Mrs. Viola Webb spent a lot of time with Mrs. King. I saw them downtown together on several occasions.

One day Mrs. Bertha Williams and I stopped by the parsonage during our lunch hour shortly after the bombing to visit the first family. Reverend King was out. Mrs. King was home and her sister was visiting. Mrs. King was upbeat. She was very strong. Her strength helped strengthen Reverend King.

The success of the Montgomery Bus Boycott became a national story. In Massachusetts, as of October 1957, a group of whites were preparing to publish a comic book-style production of the event. Adults could ascertain from the television news and newspapers what had happened in Montgomery. White boys and girls in northern cities were unable to readily put the pieces together. I knew the Struiks who were involved in the project. Mrs. Struik wrote me a letter regarding the planned publication. I informed the pastor about it. Below is the letter I forwarded to Reverend and Mrs. King:

October 16, 1957

Dear Reverend and Mrs. King,

I would like to share with you my communication of this a.m. from Dr. Sal Ruth Struik of Belmont, Massachusetts, in which she expresses her delight in her capacity as Chairman of the Boston's Fellowship of Reconciliation Project, to organize a preview sale of the "Comic Book" about the Montgomery Story. To quote from the letter:

> It is my pleasant task to organize the preview sale of the "Comic Book" about Montgomery's valiant fight under Reverend King's inspired leadership....When I, with you, was at his (the Reverend's) door and even with the shutters down, the house looked as sacred and simple to me as Lincoln's Cabin....The book, though not yet printed, sells like hot cakes (6,400) so far.

As I read her letter concerning the book, I thought maybe the book of which Dr. Struik speaks will be similar to the series in which the Jackie Robinson Story, Sugar Chile Robinson Story, and others were disseminated to the youth of America. I am sure the youth of America will be stimulated by a story presented in the most popular and effective way of communicating with them no matter what the area of thought. Science, the most exacting field, or what have you[—]"comics" are powerful in their effective motivation.

With every good wish to both of you, I am

Very truly yours,

(Mrs.) Thelma Rice

I obtained a copy of the product when it became available. It was entitled *Martin Luther King and The Montgomery Story*. It was just like a regular comic book. Various events associated with the bus boycott were highlighted in each frame. The book contained sixteen pages and cost ten cents. I still have my copy. Over the years I have allowed local teachers to make copies from my book to circulate among the children for reading.

I recommended that the January Club be the sponsor for an annual International Chat & Chew. I borrowed the idea from the National Council of Negro Women's "International Debutante Cotillion & Divertissements" of which I was a leader as president of the Mobile Metropolitan Council. This annual event was to help people develop an appreciation and respect for other cultures. At this yearly gathering we would eat foreign dishes which we prepared. A large table in the lower level of the church would be graced with foreign and American dishes and miniature flags of various countries. The first International Chat & Chew was held on Monday, 25 November 1957, 7:00 p.m., at the church. The pastor was on a committee of four for the United States of America. That committee was responsible for preparing Alabama Creole gumbo and rice. Each year the program closed with The Prayer for All Nations. In spite of all that was going on in 1957 with Reverend King, he still found time to share with the Dexter flock in special events at the church.

Pastor King loved good food—good Southern food. Mrs. King was an excellent cook. Our pastor loved pot-luck dinners. Ladies such as Mrs. Mattie Bell, Mrs. Hattie Woods, and Mrs. Fannie Doak were the leaders.

When Pastor King wrote one of his earlier works, *Stride Toward Freedom*, tempers flew. Some individuals felt they were left out of the publication and their contributions to the struggle diminished or overlooked. However, many persons who labored were not in the inner circle that made events happen. Some persons felt that Reverend King should have focused more on the pre-King years and the work done prior to his arrival in Montgomery. Some literally felt that anybody who had done any little thing should have been included.

Sister Frances Pollard, Sister Maggie Daniels, and I were book lovers. We belonged to the Great Books Discussion Group, in which we served as leaders. This group was formed by the late Ollie L. Brown, Alabama State College veteran librarian. The group used to come together for the purpose of discussing specific publications. As concerned parishioners, Sister Pollard and I arranged for Reverend King to have a session during which he would discuss his book. I approached the pastor about the idea and he concurred. *Stride Toward Freedom* was not on the group's list to discuss. However, he was aware of the frustration of some individuals and was glad for the opportunity to address concerns. He came that evening and gave an overview of the book. Afterward there was a question and answer period. Concerned persons asked questions. Reverend King responded accordingly. Pastor King was for peace and labored to maintain a tranquil setting. He explained that no one was left out intentionally and that with a publisher not every detail and minute occurrence was acceptable. Reverend King addressed the concerns of the people; but he was not greatly disturbed by their actions. He was larger than that. He would not allow small items to throw him.

Reverend King had a high appreciation for Christian fellowship. Once Dexter Avenue Baptist Church and the Mother Church, First Baptist on Ripley Street, Reverend Abernathy's congregation, had a joint early Sunday morning service. The theme was unity. Dr. Gardner Taylor, then pastor of Concord Baptist Church, New York City, was the guest preacher.

I recall and miss even now the joy of reviewing and scrutinizing his sermons. Parishioners did not examine his sermons in a critical manner. We used to examine what he said and not how he said it. His statements were so profound and his thoughts so provoking that one could not help but ponder the message Sunday afternoon and the remainder of the coming week. I used to swap sermon notes over the telephone and in person with the late Trustee F. W. Taylor and Deacon W. D. Pettus. I still have some notes of Pastor King's sermons. However, my notes only provide me half of the joy; yet half a loaf is better than no loaf at all.

When audio tapes became popular, I turned to this method instead of note taking. I sometimes share these tapes with my sister Emmerette Christine Austin and others.

When I was unable to get to church, my counselor and "Florence Nightingale", Emmerette, supplied me with notes of Pastor King's sermons.

Emmerette was likewise supportive of our January Club, International Chat and Chew, and other church groups.

I provide below for readers my hand-written notes from three of Reverend King's sermons. These notes show what I meant when saying earlier that Reverend King did not preach the old hum-drum messages.

On 24 February 1957, just before he and Mrs. King departed for Africa to witness the birth of a new nation, Ghana, Reverend King preached from the subject "It's a Great Day to be Alive."

The points recorded in my notes are: False reliance upon which we trust will drive us back to the fundamentals. Secondly, the forces of history have thrust upon us a new neighborhood and brotherhood and inevitable interdependence—a oneness in the world—a sense of brotherhood with Accra, Gold Coast. Thirdly, he stated that a new structure of freedom and justice was being established in the universe—world-wide in scope. The fourth point was that God works through history, in which events remind us of God's omnipresence and omnipotence expressed in true essence implied in the admonition "Be still and know that I am God."

Politicians started talking about a new world order in the late 1980s. I think it is interesting to note that Reverend King suggested in 1957 that a new world order was emerging.

During the morning worship service on 14 December 1958, the title of the pastor's sermon was "Worship At Its Best." This was a provocative sermon. The pastor sought to answer the question: "What is worship at its best?" Isaiah 6 was the text used. My notes reveal that worship has a three-fold quality. First the Lord is on the throne high and lifted up. Worship begins with God. Secondly, I am His. Look inward and engage in true introspection. Thirdly, hear the command to go. Look outward. My concluding notes from that sermon are: "Hear the word and believe it. Heed the command to follow by example in work done in relation to your fellowman. Worship at its best then strengthens one's growth, relation to the God of the universe, self-examination, and discipleship relation with other human beings."

On 22 March 1959 Reverend King's sermon was entitled, "The Life of A Man Who Lived in India—Mahatma Gandhi." In this sermon the features of Gandhi were highlighted. Two texts from John's Gospel were used. They were John 10:16 and 14:12. Each is cited below:

And I have other sheep, that are not of this fold; I must bring them also, and they will heed my voice. So there shall be one flock, one shepherd.

Truly, truly, I say to you, he who believes in me will also do the works that I do; and greater works than these will he do, because I go to the Father.

First it was pointed out that by using the teachings of Jesus Gandhi achieved independence for India through non-violent means. Secondly, other great men were highlighted who resisted evil, such as Thoreau and Tolstoy. Thirdly, Gandhi achieved absolute self-discipline. Fourth, Gandhi was possessed of the capacity for internal criticism.

In conclusion the pastor stated that "Gandhi was a man in the world yet not of the world. The world does not like people like Jesus of Nazareth, Gandhi, and Lincoln."

This sermon underscored the inclusiveness of God and presence of Christ for all humanity. Christ is available to all. The choice rests with "whosoever will" embrace Him.

Reverend King announced that he was resigning from Dexter Avenue Baptist Church and leaving Montgomery. Many did not want him to leave.

The Dexter family held a farewell tribute to Pastor/Preacher King. I co-authored with the late Deacon W. E. Anderson the script of "This Is Your Life." The late Mary France Fair Burks pinned an orchid corsage on Mrs. Coretta S. King.

Later the Montgomery community hosted a farewell for Reverend King. The event was held at First Baptist Church. People from the community turned out in large numbers.

After the Kings departed Montgomery, their loving, Christian, caring spirit remained a hallmark. In later years my sister, Emmerette, and the eldest member of the Austin clan, stopped at the Kings' home in Atlanta when returning from a vacation in New England. Reverend King was out of town. Mrs. King was home. Emmerette told me of the warmth and cordiality of Mrs. King.

The press often said all kinds of things about Reverend King. Much of what was said would have led some individuals to initiate a law suit and sue. However, Reverend King never took anyone to court on any account. He always turned the other cheek. This is the Pastor King and preacher I remember with great respect.

Mrs. Myrtle Pless Jones

My husband and I lived in Africa before moving to Montgomery. My husband was from Union Springs, Alabama, and was familiar with Dexter Avenue Baptist Church. We joined Dexter Avenue Baptist Church after returning from Africa.

Reverend King was a superb preacher with a tremendous vocabulary. Reverend King was full of humor.

He spoke to me one day before a church-sponsored baby contest and said of Yolanda, his firstborn: "She is the apple of my eye."

Reverend King started the birth month clubs. One of my earliest and fondest recollections of a birth month club event was a baby contest sponsored by the May Club. The event was held in June 1956 at the church.

My daughter and first born, Bobbetta, was in the contest. She was about two and a half years old at the time. The Kings' first born, Yolanda, was also a participant.

Several other mothers who are still members of Dexter had babies in the contest.

The baby contest was a fund-raising event. The child whose sponsor turned in the highest amount was declared the winner. I have a photograph from that occasion which I keep with my other family treasures from that era. Some of the other mothers who had children in the contest that year and appear in the picture are: Mrs. Rebecca Stringer (now Holbert) and son, Arthur, Jr. (deceased); Mrs. Mary Jo Smiley and daughter, Lynn; Mrs. Bertha Williams and son, Richard; Mrs. Constance Frazier and son, Severne, Jr.

Who won the contest? Yolanda King was the winner.

An article appeared in a Sunday edition of the *Montgomery Advertiser* newspaper shortly after the contest. I still have the article. It is recorded below. The article gives some insight about the month clubs and church events during Reverend King's pastorate:

Baby Yolanda King Wins Club Sponsored Contest

Baby Yolanda Denise King was the winner in the church-wide baby contest sponsored by the month clubs of the Dexter Avenue Baptist Church. Sponsored by the August club headed by Mrs. Beulah Parker Brewer, the winner reported a total of $645.60, and was awarded a cash prize of $25. The August Club won the club prize of $100. The winner is the daughter of the Rev. and Mrs. M. L. King, Jr.

Second prize winner was Lynn Smiley, winsome daughter of Dr. and Mrs. Emmett L. Smiley and sponsored by the December Club, Mrs. J. H.

Gilchrist, president. She reported $206.70. Winning third prize was Sadie Jo Dennard, daughter of Mr. and Mrs. C. L. Dennard and sponsored by the October Club headed by Mrs. Sadie Cromartie. The prizes were presented by Dr. M. L. King, Jr., who lauded all the contestants and their sponsors and expressed appreciation to all friends of the church who helped to make the total of $2,087.25.

Listed in order of rank are the remaining contestants and their sponsors: Arthur Stringer, Jr., $178.91, April Club, Mrs. Jo Ann Robinson, president; Marielle Smiley, $158.69, June Club, Dr. Zelia Evans, president; Howard Ballou, $148.75, January Club, Mrs. Thelma Austin Rice, president; Bobetta Jones, March Club, Mrs. Essie Smart, president, $140.00; Severne Frazier, Jr., February Club, Dr. W. E. Anderson, president, $126.15; Richard Williams, July Club, Miss Katie Lewis, president, $113.51; Eric Renard Davis, $64.95, September Club, Mrs. R. E. Harris, president; Lawrence Jones, $62.50, May Club, Mrs. Queen A. Tarver, president; and Isaac King, Jr., $36.50, November Club, Norman Walton, president.

A delightful program by the young people was presented under the direction of Miss Marguerite Moore and Mrs. Louvenia Herring; with the message delivered by Homer McCall, who spoke on "Youth and Democracy."

Other program participants included Misses Carolyn Motley, Myrtle Sankey, Peggy Ann Taylor, Patricia Herring, Thayer Wilson, Bessie Nelms, Alfreda Dean. Also James Draper, Gary Herring, and Dr. M. L. King, Jr.

The contest was directed by a special committee headed by J. T. Brooks and including R. D. Nesbitt, C. T. Smiley, J. H. Gilchrist, Richmond Smiley, Mrs. Thelma S. Morris, and Mrs. John Fulgham (Helen).

On another occasion we had an afternoon tea. One of the month clubs hosted a fellowship gathering. I allowed my family's heirloom silver coffee and tea service to be used that afternoon. I got the tea service from North Africa. Reverend King thought it was a thing of beauty. He rubbed it and expressed his admiration: "This is a beautiful tea service."

Reverend King went to Africa himself once. He always shared his experiences with us. When he returned from Africa, Reverend King brought his good friend and ally Reverend Ralph Abernathy a pair of sandals from the continent.

Reverend King had a tremendous sense of humor.

Mrs. Jimmie P. Walton

I first met Reverend King at Alabama State College. My husband, Norman, was a professor at that institution and a member of Dexter Avenue Baptist Church. He was escorting Reverend and Mrs. King around the campus. I was in the campus swimming pool, when my husband introduced me to the Reverend and Mrs. King.

I was not a member of Dexter Avenue Baptist Church at the time Dr. King was called to be the pastor. I had not been baptized either, though I was brought up in the church. After listening to this preacher, I walked down the aisle one Sunday following the sermon. I do not recall the sermon, but I do remember the invitational hymn. I moved toward Reverend King, who was standing down by the altar, as the choir and congregation sang "Just As I Am, Without One Plea."

It was, and is still, customary in Baptist churches for a candidate for baptism to tell why he or she wanted to join the church. Dr. King said to me: "You do not have to tell anybody why you want to join the church. You do not have to get yourself ready, just come as you are."

He had been the pastor about a year at this time.

Around 1958 three of my four children were baptized by Reverend King. The children had attended summer vacation Bible school in July of that year. In early August a closing ceremony for vacation Bible school was held. All of the boys and girls who attended were assembled in the basement of the church. Reverend King was present. When came time for the pastor's remarks, Reverend King quoted from the gospel of Matthew:

"...Jesus said, 'Let the children come to me, and do not hinder them; for to such belongs the kingdom of heaven.'"

The pastor stretched out both arms and waited to receive any of the boys and girls who would come forward and commit their lives to Christ. My daughter was about six years old. She began to move toward the minister. Her surprised older brothers, ages eleven and thirteen, tried to hinder her. Reverend King said in a calm pastoral inviting tone: "Let her come." Then he said something to this effect to the two brothers: "You boys might want to come with her."

They followed their sister. Dr. King related well to children.

Our sons and daughter were at the church with other caring adults and recounted the episode when they came home. Their father and I never pushed them to join the church, but as parents were elated with the news. All three were later baptized by the pastor. All of my children are grown and involved in various vocations. However, we still laugh about that episode.

36

My boys were in the Crusaders. It was a church group for boys. Meetings were held from house to house on Sunday afternoon. The group met at my house one Sunday on the campus of Alabama State. Dr. King, as he tried to do each Sunday the lads gathered, stopped by the house and spoke words of encouragement to the boys.

Dr. King was a grand preacher. You always got something out of his sermons. Just the sound of his voice could keep you interested.

The pastor's home was often the gathering place for church groups to meet. We often went to the parsonage to meet with the Young Matrons. When he was passing through and the ladies of the church would be meeting, Dr. King would always stop and chat.

Reverend King was always pleasant to talk to. He made you feel at ease. I thought highly of him and was saddened by his departure. He was a very caring pastor and was interested in everybody. Dr. King was a down-to-earth person. Some people say he was a saint. I do not mean to be disrespectful, but I saw him as a person and that is how he acted with us. That is how I will always remember him.

Mr. Robert D. Nesbitt, Jr.

I was most active at Dexter Avenue Baptist Church when Dr. Vernon Johns was the pastor. Reverend Johns' oldest son and I were the best of friends. When Dr. King was called to be the pastor of Dexter Avenue, I was away in college at Fisk University. My father, Robert Nesbitt, Sr., was a deacon at Dexter. I came home on some weekends and during the summer for a while. I became acquainted with Dr. King as a local pastor before the movement commenced and he became recognized as one of the giants in the land.

As a young college man, I was extremely impressed with Reverend King. Usually people get uptight around ministers, at least they did in those days. Dr. King was not the type of minister that made one feel uncomfortable. He would never embarrass an individual, but always said what needed to be stated. He would tell you the truth, if you needed to hear it. Reverend King would never let a person do anything that would have embarrassed the individual, our church, or the pastor.

Reverend King was very knowledgeable and highly intellectual. I could tell he was well read. However, he carried himself in a simple humble manner. I felt comfortable around him because, unlike older ministers, Pastor King did not preach down to people. Young people and college students could get on board with him. Dr. King preached all around you and to you.

Reverend King was young compared to other ministers I knew at that time. He was my senior by about six years. Though young, King carried himself in a way that commanded the respect of the congregation. Everybody loved him. He made people feel at ease. Above all he was genuine. You could say what you wanted to say. Dr. King did not put anybody down. His youthful appearance and young age were not hindrances. The young preacher was always in control. He never attempted to tower over others, talk loud, or do anything to secure his position. Pastor King was sure of himself.

Dr. King loved everybody. He had more compassion than any preacher I have ever met. People did not always understand him. However, once they talked with Dr. King and understood what he was saying those individuals changed. Dr. King prided himself on helping others.

Pastor King seemed to have had a hot line to heaven. He always thought matters through and never rushed a decision. If he gave you an answer, you could take it seriously. He was concerned about things that other people and preachers were not concerned about.

Dr. King's preaching was prophetic. It was as though he had seen all the events before they transpired. He said certain situations would develop and in time the events occurred. His sermons were spellbinding and spiritually uplifting. I believe that had Dr. King been the pastor of another congregation there would have been more shouting and rejoicing during worship.

King was a God-sent man. He was always there to talk and give advice. His wisdom exceeded his age. Even the older members of the church sought the advice of the young pastor before making decisions. Senior members valued his advice also. One would not have expected this from such a young minister, but that was Reverend King. His style was laid-back, but he was moving fast. It was as if he was working twenty-four hours a day.

He spent a lot of time reading. He was abreast of world events and that was evident. He could dialogue on any subject.

As a young college student, I was impressed with Dr. King's manner of dress. He was always very neat and in style. I thought he was sort of a trend setter. He looked the part of a contemporary man of the day, but maintained his clerical decorum.

Deacon John Fulgham

I grew up in the church and was baptized in the 1930s between the ages of twelve and fourteen. I grew up in Northport, Alabama, which is just across the bridge from Tuscaloosa. I was used to shouting and hollering during a worship service, as well as to a fire-and-brimstone sermon.

I joined the military and went off to war. My military career lasted from 1942-1945. I traveled to several places and grew and developed. I returned to Alabama after separating from the military. What I had experienced during my travels in the army was not what I encountered upon returning home. I returned to an environment that was small, more narrow, and less exciting.   I entered Tuskegee Institute, Tuskegee, Alabama.

After successfully completing my studies, I relocated to Montgomery. I united with Dexter Avenue Baptist Church.

Reverend Vernon Johns was the pastor. I saw something different in Reverend Johns. He wanted Black people to own stores, support each other, do for themselves, and become independent. Reverend Johns would shake the pews up with his language.

After Reverend Johns left, Reverend King came a few years later. I began to observe him. Reverend King was different, even more so than was Reverend Johns. He was a great orator. He made you listen. You had to sit still and give an ear to Reverend King. One could not move when Reverend King was preaching. This preacher had something to say. He could deliver loud and forceful like the old Black preacher, yet Reverend King had a different style. Reverend King abandoned pulpit antics, acrobatics, and crooning. His was a refined yet spirit-filled type of preaching. It was a high type of preaching, yet the every day man or woman could grasp the content of every sermon.

When the bus boycott started, I was not a deacon. I attended church regularly. I continued to be impressed with Reverend King's ministry. After the bus boycott commenced, people started coming to hear him preach.

After the movement had been going on for sometime, I noticed that my pastor was under much stress. The leadership position, as the world knows, fell to him. A friend of mine, William Martin of First Baptist Church, in Montgomery, and I decided to take Reverend King to a basketball game one night. William and I coached at George Washington Carver Senior High School in Montgomery.   I made the necessary arrangements and coordinated with pastor. We went by Reverend King's house that night and picked him up.

Reverend King was glad to be out that evening and I could tell. He was very relaxed. The movement had kept him busy and he had been closed in for quite sometime. He was glad to be around the students and ordinary people in an ordinary situation. At that time Reverend King was still a relatively young man himself, having been out of college not very long. I am sure it was his alma mater, Morehouse College, from Atlanta, playing Alabama State College that night at Dunn Arena on the campus. He walked naturally and casually with me and Martin. We filed into the arena just as the rest of the crowd did. People were not demanding his attention on this occasion. There was no media coverage, reporters asking questions, or cameras flashing in the arena. Nobody knew he was coming. How many people would have expected to see him at a college basketball game? If a person was not close to him, he or she would not have known that it was Reverend King.

Reverend King enjoyed himself to the fullest. The game was exciting. Dr. King was cheering, smiling, and supporting his favorite team like everyone else. Without question he was relieved being among the crowd. Much of the stress that had been mounting found an avenue of escape.

Following the basketball game, we took him home. I let him out in front of the parsonage. "I truly enjoyed myself," he said getting out of the car.

"We are glad you did, Reverend," William and I replied.

"If you have time on another occasion, we will take you to another game," I said.

Reverend King said he would like that. I would have also, but there was not another occasion. We never made it to another basketball game. His schedule became busier and more demands were made upon his time.

One day Reverend King approached me in the basement of the church and said: "Brother John, I think you will make a good deacon for Dexter."

Stunned by his remark I answered: "Well, Reverend, I am a football coach. You know how we coaches are when trying to win. Our language sometimes is not so good, if you know what I mean." The Reverend King assured: "I understand what you are saying. Nevertheless, you seem to live a Christian life."

I did not commit when asked. Reverend King brought the subject up on two or three later occasions. Finally I agreed to accept the position. The pastor smiled and congratulated: "I am glad you decided to accept."

Reverend King approached three others about this same time about becoming deacons. They were Julius Alexander, Roscoe Williams, and John Blair. Those three are now deceased. We had several meetings/training sessions with Reverend King. He told us his expectations and explained the role of a deacon to us.

After being ordained, I would go with the pastor to take communion to the sick and shut-in members. We would meet at the church, then I would drive. At this time I had a better grasp of the city than did Reverend King. We would talk in the car en route to the homes. His conversation was very refreshing. He would ask:

"How is everything at work?" "How is your team doing?"

When we entered the home of a sick member who was to be served communion, Reverend King would introduce himself or greet the person and then introduce or acknowledge me. For the home Holy Communion service he would read a scripture, and pray, following which communion was served. After serving communion, it was his practice to sit for a short while, rather than exit immediately, and talk. He made the sick feel good.

After the movement started, Reverend King's commitment to Dexter remained high. The church continued to support the National Baptist Convention, USA, Inc. Representatives from the Dexter congregation were chosen annually to attend the Convention's yearly Sunday School Congress, Baptist Training Union meeting, and National Convention. These ecclesiastical gatherings were held in different cities each year. Dexter Avenue Baptist Church sent two men, two women, three boys and three girls each year. I drove the church vehicle, a station wagon, to the meetings, transporting the ten individuals.

Reverend King wanted the youth involved in church activities. When the youngsters/teenagers attended the meetings it gave them an opportunity to visit different cities, to which under ordinary circumstances they would not have journeyed, as well as meet new people.

I remember driving to Buffalo, New York, Dallas, Texas, and Omaha, Nebraska. One year our pastor was the keynote speaker at the National Baptist Convention. His presence was captivating to the thousands gathered and they were excited about hearing him. Of course, our excitement did not equal that of the audience because we heard Reverend King preach regularly.

The movement had commenced and driving myself and the nine others to those annual meetings became a challenge. The station wagon had in bold script on the side—Dexter Avenue Baptist Church, Montgomery, Alabama. Everybody in the country knew this was the church where Martin Luther King, Jr., was the pastor. Churches and pastors, of course, were the leaders in the movement. Whenever I stopped for gas or drove through a town there was reason for concern. A person had to drive through almost every town and halt at every stoplight back then because interstates were not as popular as they are now.

The year the National Baptist Convention was held in Dallas I had to take creative cautious measures to protect my riders. I preferred to drive at night. I could make better time and we were not as visible. One night in a state in the deep South I was tired. There were no hotels available for Black travelers. I did not want to just pull off on the side of the road. It was impossible to determine what would happen or who would approach the station wagon and harm us. I found a graveyard, drove deep in the location, turned off the lights and engine, and prepared to retire. One of the adults inquired: "Brother John, why are you stopping in the graveyard?"

"We are safer here than any place I can think of," I replied and asked: "Who is going to bother us? Certainly not the people who are here."

It was not that bad everywhere and all white people were not mean to us. I recall stopping in another southern state coming from another church convention. I pulled up to the gas pump and waited to be serviced. Other white motorists came up after me and the attendant served each of them. I did not know how far the next gas station was and felt compelled to wait. After numerous cars came and departed, a big white gentleman, the manager, I imagine, came out. I had no idea what was about to take place. He said in a heavy southern drawl to the attendant: "Gas this man's car up and don't serve anybody else until he is taken care of."

I guess the big fellow had been standing inside watching events outside. I thanked him, paid for the gas, and we left.

I recall stopping for gas on another occasion and had the scare of my life. Two of the girls jumped out of the car as soon as I came to a halt at the gas pump. They had to use the restroom. The pair did not wait for either of the adult women to accompany them. A few moments later the girls came out of the restroom and I observed a white gentleman looking at them. I read his eyes. I had seen such looks before. Immediately I concluded what was the problem. The girls had gone into a restroom that had on the door "Whites Only." We put them in the station wagon. I explained to them that they must have one of the women go with them from that point onward. I have often wondered over the years what would have happened to all ten of us had a mean-spirited person driven up and seen those girls. God is merciful.

I never told Reverend King about any of these encounters. He was a son of the South, as was I, and knew what was happening. None of the above encounters would have surprised him.

The Montgomery Bus Boycott Movement came to a successful completion, but by that time Reverend King's reputation had spread. The demands placed upon him had increased and were still mounting. He felt the need to devote more time to the mission. It was hard, if not impossible, for him to be the pastor of Dexter and do all he was involved in. Anyone could see his labors were expanding. I truly hated to see him leave. He was my pastor and friend.

People are always talking about miracles. If I were asked to describe a miracle, I would recount the Montgomery Bus Boycott. That was a miracle. Reverend King was able to solidify several forces for a common good. Prior to his arrival in Montgomery these forces for whatever reason could not be brought together on a permanent basis. Nobody ever imagined that the Black population of this community could be galvanized and their dreams, goals, and ambitions cemented, thus providing them a common solid foundation on which they could march and sing their way to freedom.

Mr. Warren Brown

I attended another church, but went to Dexter to hear Reverend Vernon Johns one Sunday. I was so impressed with his preaching that I started attending worship service at Dexter Avenue Baptist Church regularly. My vocation was that of a barber. I had two young men who were learning to cut hair working with me at the shop. Both were students at Alabama State College. The two students heard Dr. Johns preach and all three of us started going to Dexter regularly.

I must talk about Reverend Johns first because I think his actions and principles helped pave the way for what Reverend King was able to accomplish. Some of the men in the church exerted a great deal of influence over previous pastors. However, they could not break Dr. Johns. If anything, it was the reverse. Reverend Johns was a hot-tempered individual. He could not have led the movement.

Reverend Johns was running ahead of the pack in his day. There are several episodes and encounters involving him to which I can personally attest. Reverend Johns sat in my barbershop and told me numerous stories about himself. Many of the incidents that occurred in Montgomery other people alive now know about and remember.

There was an exclusive men's store in Montgomery called Fannins. Most Black men shopped there. There were a few chairs in the store, but Black men were not allowed to sit in them. Reverend Johns went to Fannins and purchased a suit. He wrote a check for the suit and gave it to a white clerk. The clerk took the check and wrote across the top—Vernon Johns, sounding out his name.

"Can I have that check back?" Dr. Johns asked.

The white clerk gave it to him and he tore it up in front of the individual.

"You don't call me Vernon Johns," he reprimanded. "You don't know me well enough to call me Vernon Johns. Get Fred Fannins," Johns demanded.

Fred Fannins was the owner.

On another occasion Reverend Johns got on the city bus, paid his money, and was instructed to move to the back. He would not ride at the back of the bus. Reverend Johns demanded a refund. There was a disturbance of sorts on the bus. Reverend Johns got off. He recounted the episode to me later and added: "I saw the ugliest woman that day on the bus. I could not forget that face. I saw her a few days later and asked, 'What did they say about me after I got off of the bus?' She laughed, 'he-he-he-he-he.' I said to her, 'I did not ask you about "he-he-he-he." I asked what did they say after I got off of the bus.' She told me, 'They said you ought to knowed better.'"

Reverend Johns told me about an incident involving himself in a town in Virginia: "I was passing by a store one day and through the window saw a white man abusing a Black woman. I went inside to her rescue and defended the woman. I took it up. I talked about that white man's mama. You know if I talked about his mama I was ready to fight. I knew I could have been killed, but I was ready to lay my life down for the lady. Well, the next day I went past that same store and," he said in a voice of astonishment, "I saw that same heifer standing in there."

Reverend Johns would say what was on his mind. One Sunday Dr. Johns was standing in the pulpit. Dr. Trenholm, who was the president of Alabama State College at the time, entered the church. Dr. Trenholm started walking to a pew. Dr. Johns said out loud: "I see Dr. Trenholm is here today paying his annual visit."

Dr. Johns came by the barbershop selling watermelons one day.

"How many do you want?" he asked all who were in the shop.

"I don't have any money," one or two of us said.

We really did not have any funds.

He retorted: "I didn't ask how much money you have. I ask how many do you want."

"How much are they?" someone called out.

"Fifty cents," was the answer.

A young man in the shop from Bruton, Alabama, said: "In Bruton I can buy a watermelon like that for thirty-five cents."

Before the Bruton resident could end his sentence Reverend Johns replied: "In the Philippines they burn mahogany for fire wood, but mahogany is high in the United States."

That was the kind of mind Dr. Johns had.

The television special of his life portrays Reverend Johns as something close to a bum, in my opinion. However, he was nothing like the portrayal. None of the church officers would have spoken to Dr. Johns as they do in several scenes on television.

There is a scene in the Vernon Johns story where he was summoned by the city fathers because he put his sermon title, "Is It Right To Kill Negroes?" on the bulletin screen in front of the church. All persons walking or driving past the church along Dexter Avenue would have seen it.

Reverend Johns was instructed to report to one of the city authorities. Shortly after this event, my pastor recounted the episode for me one day while I was cutting his hair.

Reverend Johns said that several local white preachers were present. They had also been invited. They were not there to support Reverend Johns. The city solicitor said to Dr. Johns: "Don't you know that a sermon title like that can incite a riot?"

Reverend Johns replied: "The Lord gives me my sermons. I preach what God tells me to preach. My sermons are divinely inspired."

Reverend Johns said the white preachers present were nodding their heads affirmatively as he spoke.

Reverend Johns would go to the pool hall and talk to people. He never played pool.

"I go where people are. I get some of my sermons out of the pool room," I recall him saying one day.

Reverend Johns wanted Black people in Montgomery to be independent, do for themselves, and not beg white people for anything. He formed a co-op in Mobile Heights on Edgemont. He wanted Black people to bring their goods and support each other and buy from each other. He would say regarding his race: "You will never be anything because you are consumers."

"The Negro will send his soul to hell to save his hide, and his hide is not worth it." Dr. Johns often said.

Dr. Johns had a hot temper and he knew it. He could not have headed the movement. He would have gotten people killed. There was a businessman in Dexter Avenue Baptist Church named Mr. P. M. Blair. Reverend Johns said to me one day: "If I had Blair's personality and my sense, I could get some things done."

Following Reverend Johns' departure and an interim period, Reverend King came to Dexter. I continued to go regularly. I enjoyed Reverend King's preaching. He uttered phrases that had never been heard. I have heard nothing like them since him.

I do not know how he found out about my barber shop. Perhaps some of the men in the church told him. The young Dexter pastor would come down every Monday morning for his weekly haircut. His home was near enough for him to take a casual stroll to the shop, if he desired. He knew that I worshipped frequently at Dexter. The men in the shop saw greatness in Reverend King long before the movement started.

On several Monday mornings the young pastor teased me saying: "Brother Brown, when I opened the doors of the church yesterday, I expected to see you and Sister Brown come down the aisle."

I was really impressed with the young clergyman. I said on one occasion: "Well, Reverend, I always heard a person is supposed to join the church and not the preacher. If I joined now, I would be joining up with you. Furthermore, you are young and full of life. You will be moving on."

He laughed and countered: "Where am I going?"

I came from a rural section about eight miles from Montgomery. My wife and I were still going out to the home church, Macedonia Baptist, sometimes. We discussed joining Dexter. After Reverend King had been here a while, we joined Dexter Avenue Baptist Church.

The protest movement started. I was not a part of the protest demonstrations. I did not march with Reverend King. Most Black people in Montgomery rode the bus in those days. There were several seats on the front of the bus reserved for white people. Black riders paid their fare and had to move to the rear of the bus even when seats were available at the front. Mrs. Parks was arrested. This was not the first incident of this sort, but was the one that brought events to a head. Her husband was a barber also. The way I understood events the people wanted the seating on the bus to be on a first-come-first-served basis—nothing more and nothing less.

Initially the boycott was for one day. It was the Black community's way of saying they resented the treatment of the white establishment toward them. The bus used to come right past my house about every eight to ten minutes in the morning. I looked out each time I heard the sound of a bus. Many white people thought there would be Black workers who would ride. Motorcycle police followed the buses to make sure that any Black workers who wanted to board could do so without fear. However, no Black workers wanted to board the buses. Each time I peered out of the window, upon hearing an engine, I saw an empty bus. Things went well that day. Another mass meeting was held the next night and it was decided that the boycott should be continued. Reverend King was still asking that passengers assume seating on the bus on a first-come-first-served basis. City officials would not yield.

The night the parsonage was bombed was a trying evening in the Montgomery community. The word of what happened spread fast. I do not know till this day how the news circulated so swiftly. I rushed to the pastor's home on Jackson Street. Numerous persons were standing in the yard. It was not just Reverend King's church members in the yard. People from throughout the community had come together, whether they attended Dexter Avenue Baptist or not. Reverend King had become a community pastor of sorts. The people in the yard were upset, teary eyed, and angry. So was I. People had pistols, rifles, knives, sticks, and anything that could be used as a weapon. I had my .32 revolver in hand.

The fire chief, police commissioner, and mayor were on the front porch. Reverend King came out of the house and put up his hands. After he got the attention of the crowd and the noise subsided, we were assured that everyone in the house was fine. Reverend King urged us to continue to be peaceful, go home, and let the movement progress non-violently. The crowd dispersed.

However, this much I know; if an uncontrollable spirit had come over those standing in the front yard, the mayor, fire chief, and police commissioner would not have stood a chance. Only Reverend King could have spoken in such a manner that made the crowd turn and walk away peacefully.

After that incident, some of the men in the church formed a group. We took turns guarding the pastor's home. We worked in shifts. Each person sat inside by the window and peered out. I only remember one time that there was reason for concern. A car came by the house and slowed down one night. White passengers were inside. Two men from the church followed the vehicle down to the area of the capitol, but nothing became of it.

Reverend King said, after the bombing of his home: "I fear for my life."

He started talking then about the longevity of life and how that concept had to be viewed. He, like anyone else, wanted to live a long life was his confession; but there was work to be done. Reverend King knew that if he stayed the course and held to his mission he was likely to be killed. Nothing could make him turn back or abandon the work he started, not even death. He said that his often-repeated prayer was for God to give him strength to go on rather than quit.

The white people said Reverend King was a law-breaker. Reverend King said that all citizens had the right to protest against any unjust law.

Reverend King began to talk about voting and registering. He incorporated civic duties as a citizen into his sermons. It all made sense. He said the vote was a weapon.

Only a few Black residents in Montgomery were allowed to register. Many were denied the right to register for no legitimate reason.

A friend of mine, Mr. Rufus Lewis, worked hard to get Black people to register and vote. Lewis came to the barber shop on numerous occasions. After several visits, I promised him that I would go and register. We had to take a test. Another barber and I went together to register. I was able to register, but my friend was denied the right to register. He came out disappointed. We stood together in the city building. A white man was there to register. He had not done well on his examination. I do not know if every applicant took the same test. Nevertheless, this white fellow did not have the correct answers. My friend and I watched the white registrar give the white applicant the correct answers. We were standing right there looking.

As the protest continued, Reverend King told us that white people had all the weapons and firepower, and all protesting would have to be non-violent. Non-violent protest was the only chance the people stood, according to his reasoning. There was no room for, or victory through, violence.

White people had done much wrong to Black people. Reverend King explained that he was appealing to the conscience of white people. He wanted them to think about the way they had treated and were treating Black people and repent, change their attitude and thinking. The whites had the power and owned practically everything. They needed to change their views about life and Black people. It was his contention that in order for Black people to secure their rights white people had to yield and repent.

The White Citizens Council was formed. This organization tried to get all white families who had Black domestic workers to fire the latter. Working for white families was the only source of income for many domestic workers and their oppressors knew that. However, if Black domestics were fired, white females would have had to resign their employment (income), stay home, and perform the duties that their domestics were assigned. White females were not willing to quit their jobs and stay home. So the plan backfired.

Other tactics were implemented. For example, when a college graduate filled out an application to teach, one question on the form was—"Are you a member of the National Association for the Advancement of Colored People (NAACP)?" Of course, if the applicant checked yes, he or she was denied employment.

When various tactics designed by whites failed and could not be re-worked, they simply made their parting act as devastating a possible. For example, there was a swimming pool in Oak Park. Rather than allow the Black children to have access to it, the whites filled the empty receptacle with cement. That way nobody got any use out of the pool.

I remember Reverend King being jailed once. Either he could not make bail or he refused to accept bail. I think the latter was the case. When it was learned that he was out, it was asked how was his release secured. The police commissioner explained: "I let him out. I let him out because I did not want him among my inmates with his message."

Reverend King continued to come to my barber shop and I would trim his hair. He was a very modest man. He never initiated a conversation, but would always join in and talk about whatever was being discussed by the men in the shop.

Tension in the community increased. Many Black people were becoming irritated with Reverend King. They said his activities and work were making life unpleasant for them.

Some of the church members complained that the pastor was hurting their cause. Working persons were being threatened by their employers.

The old comfort zones were being disturbed. Reverend King got the word. This put the young pastor in a very awkward situation, but he was very pastoral in his resolution. Reverend King stood in the pulpit and said one Sunday: "Those who are working and have jobs might not lift a finger or say a word in support of or in defense of the movement, but they think no more of you than they do of those who are protesting. In fact, they (meaning the local white establishment) do not think as much of you as they do those who are out protesting. When it is over, whatever the outcome, you will benefit just as much as anyone else, even those who will lose their lives."

On another Sunday he announced: "I have been offered money to stop what I am doing and retire from the movement."

However, Reverend King believed in his mission and would not turn back.

I hated to see Reverend King leave Montgomery. Black people were complaining that he was hurting their cause.

When I learned that Reverend King had been assassinated, I was hurt. On the Sunday before his funeral I drove to Atlanta following church service at Dexter to view his remains. Richard Nixon was there when I arrived. I could not let Reverend King be buried without paying my last respects in some way.

I am always moved by the recollection of his words: "The ultimate measure of a man is not where he stands in moments of comfort and convenience, but where he stands at times of challenge and controversy."

I have a photograph of him in my barbershop. Each time I look at it many pleasant memories come to mind.

Ms. Verdie Davie, Age 97

I met Reverend King the first Sunday he came to preach at Dexter Avenue Baptist Church. The pulpit was vacant at the time. I drove the custodian to the church earlier that Sunday morning. The two of us were in the church. The preacher for the day arrived about 9:15 a.m. He introduced himself to me: "Good morning, I am Martin Luther King, Jr., from Ebenezer Baptist Church in Atlanta. I am going to preach here today."

He inquired about the order of events.

"We have Sunday School at 9:30, worship at 11:00, and Baptist Training Union at 5:00 p.m.," I outlined.

I looked at him and said to myself, "He would make us a good pastor." I liked the way he presented himself. He talked intelligently and had a nice voice. I could tell he was well educated. He was humble even on the first occasion. He arrived early at the church, but did not try to take over.

Reverend King preached a moving sermon. The congregation was very impressed with him. He probably could have been elected the pastor that day. After Reverend King visited with us and preached several more times, the congregation voted for him to be the pastor. There was not a dissenting vote. He was young, but we immediately overcame that obstacle. Reverend King was in his twenties, but acted far more mature.

He took his pastoral duties seriously. After being called to serve Dexter Avenue Baptist Church, the parsonage was not ready to be occupied. Nevertheless, he came on to Montgomery. Reverend King boarded with a Dexter family until the parsonage was ready. He stayed with Mrs. Sally Madison and family on Grove Street.

Reverend King was a great organizer. Reverend King organized the Church with clubs. When he came to be the pastor, all we had was the Sunday school, morning worship, Baptist Training Union, and the official boards, deacon and trustee.

Dexter Avenue Baptist Church was composed of numerous educators. Many of the Alabama State College faculty, as well as the president of the college, attended Dexter. The clubs were organized to get all the people together. All of the people—the well-educated and the not-so-well-educated. For example, we had the birthday club. You belonged to the club of the month in which you were born and your educational background carried no weight. If you were born in March, you were in the March Club no matter what your educational attainment. I liked the idea of him trying to bring the church together.

Love was Reverend King's theme. That word *agape* he dwelt on. Reverend King tried to get us to grasp the full meaning of that word. He often spoke and preached about that unconditional love. He urged people to work for a living, be honest, and have their own homes.

Reverend King lifted us up and got us to knowing all those big words. He made us want to learn and read more. In his sermons, he would use some big words. We would go home and look them up, but the messages were still plain. You left church each Sunday having gotten the gist of the sermon, but you still wanted to know the definition of some of the terms.

People being educated was a concern of his. He often said: "Send your family to school. Educate your children. Every man should take care of his family."

He preached about education. He told parents to send their children to school so they could develop intellectually. When grown, they could stand their ground and not have to be an Uncle Tom.

He helped remove ignorance and fear from our minds.

Reverend King could handle folk. He ruled with love. He never forced you to do anything, but when he spoke about love you succumbed.

Oooohhhh my, could some of the members call his name. They would walk right behind him, on his heels literally saying: "Dooccctttor King, such and such."

They would sound his name out with such love, affection, admiration, and respect. The people at Dexter could call his name like no others in the world could do.

We had no church constitution back then. Pastor King ruled by love and with the Bible. He was truthful. When Martin Luther King, Jr., said something, it made you want to respond.

Reverend King was not flashy. He was an ordinary, down-to-earth Christian gentleman. He never changed. He was not wishy-washy. If he ever had a good thought, you could not change him.

Reverend King never boasted that he was the pastor. He was secure in his position. He was a man sent from God. Oh, my, he knew the Bible and preached the Bible. Love, Love, Love, he preached.

After the movement started, Reverend King did not visit parishioners as much. People were after him. Nevertheless, he visited those who needed his pastoral attention and cared for the flock as best he could, even when opponents were trying to destroy him.

The male members of the church would sometimes leave Dr. King in their homes so he could rest. He could not repose at home. The telephone was always ringing. Sometimes people needed his help. Other times threats were being voiced.

Our young pastor was full of life. I can see him laughing now. He was never too busy to stop and talk to a person. I think of him daily.

Mrs. Maggie Shannon

I did not hear the sermons Reverend King preached as a candidate for the Dexter pulpit. I first heard him after he was called to be the pastor.

I remember the first time I saw him. It was during a Sunday morning worship service. Reverend King was to deliver the sermon. Someone sitting next to me, I do not recall who, remarked in a soft voice: "I wonder what that little boy can do."

It must have been that person's first time seeing him also.

"Give him a chance," I answered, "give 'im a chance."

After the sermon, I said: "He has it. He is alright."

I am sure the person who asked me that question felt the same.

Dr. King was a great speaker. He preached the Gospel. It was Bible preaching. His voice would go all over you. His words had power.

Pastor King was full of life. He was very understanding and would always listen to you. You could tell him your troubles. When sick, the pastor came to see you. He used to walk to my house and talk to me. Several times I had to have him come by and talk with my boys. My sons were at the age when they could be very disagreeable and stubborn in their ways and decisions. I had to call Reverend King to my house more than once to talk to those boys.

The King family was a delight. Reverend King had my sons in the Crusaders for Boys. Mrs. King used to come by and pick up my daughters for missionary meetings at her house.

Dr. King had a sweet mind and a fine sense of humor. I have never seen anyone like him. Every time you were around him or engaged in a conversation you found something to laugh about. I had seven boys and three girls. Reverend King used to tease me about the size of my family.

He was good with children. On Sunday he would invite the boys and girls in the congregation to come to the altar and would pray for them. This was his practice before he became extremely busy with the movement.

When he learned that my daughter's birthday was on the 15th of January as was his, Dr. King laughed and said: "She is going to be a fine girl."

Reverend King performed several significant pastoral acts within my family circle. Pastor King baptized several of my children: Robert, James Edward, and Thomas Earl. He performed the marriage of my oldest son, Claude, Jr. to Pattie Davis.

Every Sunday, following the benediction, Reverend King would walk to the back of the church and stand by the door. He would shake the hand of each worshipper before that person left the church. He was a true pastor.

Reverend King was a fine Christian man and a man of faith. He told us one Sunday about a trip, during which he was on a boat with numerous others. The engine went out. The people on board were upset and frantic. He told them to remain calm and still. Reverend King said he prayed. Shortly thereafter the captain started the engine and they journeyed on.

After he had been the pastor of Dexter for sometime, you had to come to church earlier than usual to get a seat. Even those of us who were members of Dexter had to come early. The days of casually walking into the sanctuary and randomly choosing a seat were gone. Visitors from all over came to hear our pastor. It got to the point where people just wanted to hear and see Reverend King.

After the movement started, the church was always packed on Sunday. One Sunday a white gentleman and his daughter were worshipping with us. They were sitting near me. The church was filled to capacity. The man wanted his four or five year old daughter to see Reverend King. He asked me: "Would you please hold my daughter up so she can get a good look at Dr. King?"

I obliged him.

I will confess that I did not participate in the protest marches. I had children. I could not envision them being left in this world motherless, if it came to that. I did attend several mass meetings. The first one I attended was at Day Street Baptist Church. Reverend King would visit homes and talk to people about attending mass meetings. He was asking the people to do what he was willing to do himself.

One Sunday opponents of the movement came to Dexter Avenue Baptist Church. We had morning worship each week no matter what. The opponents remained outside of the church. They threw bricks against the structure. They were saying things such as: "We are going to kill that King."

Following the benediction, worshippers learned they could not leave the church. A disagreeable crowd had gathered. Military men from nearby Maxwell Field, now Maxwell Air Force Base, only a short drive from Dexter, were brought in to escort us out of the church. We were escorted out twelve persons at a time. The military personnel gave protection to each person or family until all were in their automobiles. That was a trying Sunday. Opponents, however, were disappointed. Reverend King did not preach at Dexter that Sunday. He was away.

Reverend King resigned as the pastor of Dexter. Several years later he returned to the State of Alabama to lead the Selma to Montgomery March. Reverend King was scheduled to address the marchers in front of the capitol at the conclusion of the trek. I worked for a white family. The lady of the household where I worked said to me: "Maggie, when you go home today, don't go through town as you usually do. They are gathering down there and it could be trouble."

She was concerned about my safety. She knew the church I attended and Reverend King had been my pastor in earlier years. I told her: "My pastor is going to speak to the people and I am going to be there to support him today when he speaks."

I do not remember all that Reverend King said to the marchers who had returned from Selma. However, I remember him saying, and the crowd welcoming his words: "Governor Wallace, you said it could not be done, but here we are."

I was always moved by the events Reverend King would recount regarding his activities. I remember him telling how the authorities in Birmingham sprayed him with water and put the dogs on him and others.

Reverend King was a great man.

Mr. Nelson Malden

I left Pensacola, Florida, and came to Montgomery, Alabama, in 1952. Alabama State College was the nearest institution of higher learning. I was accepted there as a student. Florida A&M was in my home state, but was a greater distance away.

My oldest brother, Cleveland, came to Montgomery earlier. Cleveland got his hair cut at College Hill Barber Shop. He learned of an opening for a barber. He told my other older brother, Spurgeon, about the position. Spurgeon left home and came to Montgomery. In 1952, Spurgeon joined the United States Army. However, he got me on at College Hill Barber Shop with Mr. Warren Brown. I arrived as Spurgeon departed. I was given Spurgeon's chair at College Hill.

I started attending Dexter Avenue Baptist Church during Reverend Vernon Johns' tenure. I came to town near the end of Reverend Johns' ministry. He used to get his hair cut at College Hill Barber Shop also. Mr. Warren Brown, the proprietor of College Hill, took me to Dexter. The people were nice, but the membership was not that large. In fact, most of the professional Black men—teachers, principals, dentists, and physicians—got their hair cut at College Hill Barbershop. Many of those professional men attended Dexter Avenue Baptist Church.

Reverend Johns had an awesome memory. He memorized long passages of scripture. His sermons were well tied together. He did not ramble. He loved poetry and included it in his sermons. Reverend Johns' delivery was great. He would dramatize a great deal.

Reverend Johns was his own man. He would sometimes wear a wrinkled suit in the pulpit, caring nothing for clothes. He was a different breed. One Sunday I saw the sleeve of a pajama top hanging from under the arm of his long sleeve shirt. On several occasions he was in the pulpit with no socks on.

The first time I saw Reverend King I was a student at Alabama State College. That was about 1955. I was cutting hair at the College Hill Barber Shop under the tutelage of Mr. Warren Brown. I had an 11:00 a.m. class and would cut hair until 10:35 a.m. or 10:40 a.m. My policy was never to take a customer after this time because I could not do a good job and make it to class on time. One morning a taxi pulled up and a young man got out. He was well dressed. The man wanted a haircut. It was about 10:45 or thereabouts. I looked at his head and noticed his hair was very short. I thought to myself—"I can cut his hair in just a few minutes and still get to class on time." So he got in the chair and I gave the preacher a trim.

His conversation was casual. The usual barber-customer conversation. Where are you from? How is life? etc.

I knew Reverend King before he ascended to universal prominence. He purchased a blue 1954 Pontiac. He obviously did not put much emphasis on material things. Otherwise he would have purchased a top-of-the-line car.

He was always neatly dressed. He wore top-of-the-line clothes, Stacey Adams shoes, and nice hats. He also employed the services of a local tailor.

I joined Dexter Avenue Baptist Church under Reverend King. I grew up in a Baptist Church in Pensacola. Initially Reverend King was not in the same ball park as Reverend Johns in terms of sermon delivery and impact. Johns was a seasoned preacher. When at his best, Dr. Johns could make events in a sermon come to life. Reverend King was young when he came to Dexter. He had spent many years in the classroom. He had a well of fresh thoughts. It was good, hard stuff. You could tell he was well prepared. There was never any filibustering around or ad-libbing. However, Reverend King's oratory and mass communication skills were being perfected. He could not rival Reverend Johns. Reverend Johns' sermons were singularly focused. He and his listeners stayed on the same road throughout the sermon. Reverend King's sermons were broad and philosophical.

Reverend King was still going back and forth to Boston. He had not completed his dissertation. Most of the members felt they were larger than the pastor. Reverend King faced the same encounters at Dexter that any young pastor would have faced.

He was always a people's person. Reverend King could mingle and fit in with all persons regardless of their background. However, anyone could tell that he was not just a run-of-the-mill fellow. It was very obvious that he came from a good background, fine home, and had parents of high standing. There was an air of independence about him. He was not dependent on others. Reverend King, as stated earlier, came from a good home and had supportive parents. If the need arose, he could have returned to the home of his parents at any time.

He started the month clubs at the church. My brother, Spurgeon, was in the January Club with Reverend King. Reverend King brought high-powered Black speakers to Dexter. As a young man, I was fascinated by these intellectual giants. For example, Benjamin Mays came to Dexter. On another occasion, Mordecai Johnson was a guest speaker.

One night Reverend King invited some of the young men from the college to Dr. Harding's home. Harold Carter, T. Y. Rogers, John Porter and myself were invited. However, I had the second-best hand at College

Hill Barber Shop. I declined the invitation and went to work that evening. As a college student, I needed the money. I do not know exactly what transpired that evening at Dr. Harding's. I often wonder. I think Reverend King was seeking out young men to join his fraternity—Alpha Phi Alpha Fraternity, Inc.

The other three young students, Carter, Rogers, and Porter, as young men in life made fine ministers. I feel certain Reverend King had some influence on each.

Reverend King's fame was launched on the night the first mass meeting was held at Holt Street Baptist Church. The media was there. They were not there to see Reverend King because he was not well known at that time. The Black community was not well organized during those days. The media came to see what was going to happen. The news was beamed out of Montgomery to the nation. The rest is now history.

Many of the local preachers supported Reverend King initially. Numerous other ministers from outside of Montgomery later came along and jumped on the band wagon. However, it was the local clergy who lined up behind him and got things rolling.

Reverend B. D. Lambert was some kind of preacher and one of Reverend King's devout supporters. Reverend King loved having Reverend Lambert around. The latter would get the people all excited at some of the gatherings. He would set the stage for Dr. King. Some of the men who attended the first mass meeting told me Reverend Lambert said: "My Daddy always told me the best way to kill something was to stab it in the heart. We are in the heart of Dixie and tonight we are going to stab segregation to death."

Some of the other local supporters among the clergy who rallied to Reverend King—and the number increased as time elapsed—were: Reverends Solomon Seay, Sr., B. D. Lambert, pastor of Maggie Street Baptist Church, Felix E. James, pastor of Hall Street Baptist Church, and Reverend Wilson, pastor of Holt Street Baptist Church.

While he was completing his dissertation, Reverend King met Lawrence Reddick, Ph.D. The latter was on the faculty at Alabama State College. Dr. Reddick's area of study was history. The two men formed a lasting relationship. Reddick had a small ego. He was researching the laws of Alabama and did not want his name out front. He worked quietly. That was how he did his best work.

My brother and I left Mr. Warren Brown and started our own business in 1958. The name on the window today reads as it did in that year—Malden Brothers Barber Shop. The barber shop was located where it is today at 407 South Jackson Street. Reverend King lived at 309 South Jackson.

Reverend King would go to the pool room several times a week. It was just a little place around the corner from the barbershop. I do not even remember the name of the pool hall. Come to think of it I do not believe it had a name. The place had two pool tables inside. Reverend King was good, extremely good. He could beat most of the fellows around here. He played with my late brother, Spurgeon. Only a few pool players around here could beat King.

Reverend King would walk down to the campus of Alabama State College. Most days he would stop in the shop going or returning and have a soda. He had a good rapport with young men. If there were people in the shop when he stopped, Reverend King would shake everybody's hand and say something like: "Hi, I am Martin Luther King, pastor of Dexter Avenue Baptist Church. Come by and see us sometime."

After the movement started, people started coming to Dexter in large numbers. You had to get to church early to get a seat. The year Reverend King arrived one could come to church at any time and find a seat. It was one of his goals to increase Dexter's membership. I think he wanted the church to grow and be stable in membership. When the protest was in full gear, people were packing the church every Sunday but it was his prominence that drew them.

Reverend Vernon Johns returned to Montgomery in 1958. He came by the shop. My brother, Spurgeon, had gone out of the shop for a little while. Business was slow that day. I noticed some spots on Reverend Johns' face. I offered him a mud-pack treatment. He got in the chair. It was a bittersweet visit to Montgomery for him. Reverend Johns was moved by the events that were taking place. At the same time I could tell he was a little hurt. The very transformation that was occurring was what he tried to initiate during his stay in Montgomery. There is no doubt that during his stay he set the tone and gave the people nerve.

The students at Alabama State College were very active in events. The governor of the state directed the president of the college to dismiss many of the students. However, the president held his ground and did not.

I remember one day a group of students left Alabama State College going downtown to march. The authorities stopped the students right out in front of the barbershop and would not allow them to continue. Reverend King was in Jackson, Mississippi, that day. Someone contacted him in Jackson and explained what was going on. He caught a plane and returned. The students were still in front of the barbershop being held at bay when Reverend King arrived in the community. Seeing what was transpiring, he and some of his lieutenants went to the home of Mr. Rufus Lewis for a strategy session. Mr. Lewis' home was just around the corner from the barbershop. They left Mr. Lewis' home and went to Mr.

Goldsmith's hotel and had another session. In the end, the students were allowed to proceed.

Mr. Goldsmith's establishment was only a few doors down from the barber shop. It was on the corner of Jackson and High Streets. The establishment was three stories. On the top floor was a night club. Cabarets were held on the top floor. The second floor was a hotel. A restaurant was on the ground floor.

Reverend King and his lieutenants would sometimes have meetings there. At the height of the movement college students from other states came to Montgomery. Some residents hosted students in their homes. Mr. Goldsmith's hotel was about the only hotel they could stay in. The movement received monies from supporters around the country. The incoming college students could not afford to pay for a hotel room. Some monies were used to help pay for their lodging.

The white establishment tried to make Mr. Goldsmith stop accommodating the students, but he refused. Certain officials tried to put pressure Mr. Goldsmith. There was a cabaret tax that business persons/night club owners were supposed to pay. However, it was never enforced. They got Mr. Goldsmith on the cabaret tax and closed down his business. This measure was employed against him because of his stand. There were numerous other business men in town who owned night clubs and were not paying the cabaret tax. They, however, remained in business.

Malden Brothers Barber Shop had the only public pay telephone in the immediate vicinity. Many times one of Reverend King's lieutenants would come into the shop and use the telephone to call out news. One day we discovered that the telephone in the shop was bugged.

There was a lady named Mrs. Gilmore who participated in the movement. She was a cook for a local restaurant. When her white employer found out Mrs. Gilmore was part of the protest, she was fired. She told Reverend King about it.

"Well, why don't you open up your own restaurant," he asked, challenging her. "Go into business for yourself."

Mrs. Gilmore started cooking in her home. She would buy chicken by the cases. The meals were prepared and sold at her house on Dericote Street. You could eat at the house or get a carry out. Reverend King loved to eat. He enjoyed eating at Mrs. Gilmore's. She was an excellent cook. I used to go over about 11:00 a.m. several times a week and purchase my lunch. Her home was a five-minute walk from the barbershop.

Reverend King took all of the VIPs to Mrs. Gilmore to eat when they came to Montgomery. Reverend King took Senator Robert Kennedy there to eat. Ralph Bunche was a customer. There was no telling who you would see at Mrs. Gilmore's house. Numerous news anchormen covering the movement ate there. Mrs. Gilmore sold enough plates out of her house to send all of her children through college. After all of the children were out of college, she built a new home.

History is sometimes misleading. Mrs. Gilmore's house is now a historic site. However, the house now designated as a historic site is not the house she started in. The history was in the first house. That was where all the VIPs sat and ate at one time or another. However, that house no longer exists. A vacant lot is where the historic home was located. Mrs. Gilmore's second home is less than a two-minute walk from the vacant lot.

It was my brother Spurgeon who used to have all the long philosophical debates with Reverend King in this barbershop. I recall Reverend King standing near Spurgeon's chair one day saying: "If you co-operate with injustice it will in-corporate you."

After he became famous, body guards sometimes accompanied Reverend King. One day he was walking in the vicinity of the barber shop. My brother and some other fellows said: "We see you don't have your guards walking with you today." "No," Reverend King responded, "they are not. The Lord is walking with me today."

I think he was saying that ultimately it was God who walked with and protected individuals and not persons appointed to guard them.

I think Reverend King was well aware of his youth and the unparalleled work he was doing at such a tender age. After receiving the Nobel Peace Prize, I heard him say in a public setting regarding his maturation and early years in Montgomery: "I was a boy then, but I am a man now."

The last time I saw Reverend King was one day when he came by the shop. Jesse Jackson was with him. Reverend King always enjoyed the barber shop scene and talking to people. Jesse Jackson reminded Reverend King that they had a plane to catch.

"Just let me talk a few more minutes," Reverend King said.

Reverend King decided to leave Montgomery. He said that flights went out of Atlanta more frequently and that would make traveling easier for him. I think that was an excuse. There was some truth to that. He would have been able to get out of Atlanta easier than out of Montgomery to go on speaking engagements and such. However, in carrying out his mission, Reverend King was interfering with the bread and butter of some of the folk in the church. I sensed that he wanted to remain in Montgomery.

Mrs. Althea Thompson Thomas

Six years had passed since I had been in regular Sunday morning attendance at the African Methodist Episcopal Zion Church where my family held membership for three generations.

For the first four of those six years I was the organist at another Methodist church. This church was very similar to my African Methodist Episcopal Church in tenet, liturgy, and church personality. However, I was never moved to the point of wanting to become a member.

I was an organist during my four years of college, as well as one year beyond college.

During the Spring of 1955, I was preparing for my wedding. As the month of June neared, the telephone rang more frequently. One day the telephone rang. I had no idea who was calling. "Hello," I answered.

"Hello," a male voice replied. "I am Martin King. I want to talk to you about filling the position of organist at my church."

This is probably some deep-water Baptist church I thought. I had already decided that I was not going to play for any church for a while. I was preparing to get married, spend time with my future husband and rear a family. I had already told my husband-to-be that I was not going to play for any church for some time to come. I had been serving in some music capacity in church since I was a girl.

"I am the pastor of Dexter Avenue Baptist Church," Reverend King said.

"Oh, yes sir," I said.

He had been the guest speaker at a recent commencement exercise at Alabama State College. I heard Reverend King speak on that occasion and was greatly impressed with him. I knew about the music situation at Dexter. Many of the Alabama State College music faculty assisted.

Mrs. Vernon Johns, whose husband pastored Dexter prior to Dr. King, was on the staff at Alabama State College. Mrs. Johns was a concert pianist of the first magnitude. On television she is portrayed as a woman who took music around the corner for twenty-five cents. Mrs. Johns came from a fine family. Her father was one of the presidents of Livingstone College in North Carolina.

"You have been enthusiastically recommended," Reverend King lauded.

He is just buttering me up, I said to myself.

"I want to apologize for offering you a position where you will be subordinate to someone less qualified," he explained.

I knew Dr. Brooks. His primary discipline was another field of study. However, what he lacked in musical academic credential Dr. Brooks made up for in talent and dedication. Unlike most self-taught organists, he mastered the technique of legato playing. His hymn playing was on a par with a third-year organ student in one of the fine institutions or music academies.

"I will be glad to work under Dr. Brooks."

I thought it would be easy to work under Dr. King and Dr. Brooks.

"When can you start?"

"I can start this Sunday." Dr. King was pleased with my response. Then I remembered and said: "Oh, I am getting married on Saturday. I will start the second Sunday in June."

Reverend King agreed to let me start playing on the second Sunday in June 1955. That was not going to be a problem because Wiley and I had already decided that we would not go on a honeymoon. My husband-to-be was starting graduate school. There was something about Dexter Avenue Baptist Church and the Reverend Doctor Martin Luther King, Jr., that quickened a desire in me to become an active member.

I made my desire known. Reverend King was pleased and said that I would be extended the right hand of fellowship after being baptized. Stunned for a moment and knowing that I had found the Lord many years earlier, I recalled the fact that my baptism in the Methodist Church had been by sprinkling.

For more than a week I existed in denominational limbo before determining not to let my hydrophobia stand between me and the church of my choice. (The good people of Dexter were not aware of or responsible for my having nearly drowned as a toddler and having emerged from the incident permanently afraid of water). I never discussed this fear with anyone. No one would believe how afraid I was of being immersed. Part of my fear was generated by Reverend King. It was his size. In many photographs he appears to be large. Contrary to popular belief, he was a small man. After much prayer came the day for the baptism.

Speaking of the public's belief that he was a big person, a friend in Texas called our home one evening. This was after events had really heated up in Montgomery. He said: "That big Black fellow is tearing Montgomery up."

My husband and I laughed because we knew Reverend King was not a large person. In fact, neither description articulated by our friend in Texas was accurate.

I remember the saintly, supporting countenance of Martin Luther King, Jr., as he stood in the baptistery. My hydrophobia was very real, but suddenly I felt absolute peace. The water was cool. The season was midwinter. The baptistery was deep. The spirit of the Lord was in His place. The traditional words were uttered—"In obedience to the great command and upon the confession of your faith I baptize you in the name of the Father, Son, and the Holy Spirit." I was immersed. My baptism was a deep and most gratifying experience.

At the age of twenty-three I had a very serious problem, or I thought I did. I have vainly tried to recall the particulars. Anyway, one Sunday I was very nervous and did not play well. Dr. King became aware of my uneasiness. In retrospect, I can appreciate the pastoral care of Reverend King.

I was the last person to exit the sanctuary that Sunday and shake the pastor's hand.

"Is everything all right?" he inquired, sensing something was wrong.

I could not answer because any utterance would have been accompanied by a flood of tears. I shook my head.

"Do you need to talk about it?" asked the pastor.

"Gee, I must have really been off this morning," I mused and nodded affirmatively.

We agreed on a time when I would come for counseling.

As I poured my heart out, Reverend King listened, hands clasped under his chin, index fingers supporting his cheeks (in his now popular pensive pose). I talked for approximately one hour and ended with the desperate phrase: "I can't handle it!"

When I said that, he broke his silence with three words spoken with conviction: "Yes, you can!"

This was a startling, disappointing comment. It lacked the compassion and sympathy that my aching heart (or perhaps it was bruised ego) craved at that time. I just looked at Reverend King. "Yes, you can," he continued. "Oh, I am not saying that it should have happened to you or that you should have to handle it, but you must never think that you can't handle it."

I immediately felt better. After exchanging a few more words, I thanked him for his wise counsel. As I started out, I repeated: "Yes, I can!"

Reverend King ended: "You don't have to face anything alone. Pray!"

Since that counseling session with the pastor, my personal assurance has been—"I can do anything with God's help."

Dr. King was very good with basic stuff. He did not dilly-dally around. He always came right to the point. His words were strong, but when appropriate he laced them with humor. He was not a stone face.

After the protest started, Reverend King was arrested. The photograph of him in police custody wearing a suit and wide-brim hat has appeared in many publications. He always wore those nice hats. The Sunday after the arrest the church was extremely quiet. You could hear a mouse walk on cotton. Reverend King stood up in the pulpit and broke the silence saying: "Your pastor is a jail bird."

One of the sayings that Dr. King stated frequently was: "If there is nothing in your life you will die for, you have nothing to live for."

Dexter has always been located in downtown Montgomery. When Reverend King came to be the pastor, there were a lot of houses in the vicinity of the church. In one of the homes almost next to Dexter lived a family that kept up a considerable amount of noise on Sunday. It was a white family. I don't think the family went to any church. Sunday seems to have been the day they washed the car, washed the dog and accomplished other chores.

One Sunday it was very hot. We did not have air conditioning. The windows had been raised in the church to help fresh air circulate. The noisy family was actively engaged in some task outdoors. We could hear voices yelling: "There he is." "Git 'im. Catch 'im."

I reasoned they were washing the dog.

Reverend King said: "One of you deacons go next door and ask them to tone it down. The law says it should be quiet at this hour and they know the law. I am sure they are not acting out of malice. They are probably unaware that their voices are carrying and disturbing the worship service."

I was next to the window. The bus boycott was in high gear at that time. I became very uneasy. Deacon Robert Nesbitt, Sr., went next door and spoke to the family. The noise immediately ceased.

After the movement was under way, a group of white ladies organized a Women's Council. It was integrated. I went to one meeting. Reverend King addressed the group on the subject of non-violence and passive resistance.

I listened and lifted up the following illustration to Dr. King for consideration.

"My father taught me how to drive. He told me if the car ever started skidding I should turn the wheel in the direction of the skid. The first time my car went into a skid I did the opposite. How can I be sure I will be passive when someone is unfair to me? How can I be sure I will be passive if a white person slaps my child?"

"No one knows what he or she will do in a certain situation," Dr. King commenced. "If you prepare yourself, you will probably do what you are prepared to do."

I did not march. There was no particular reason. I was on the faculty at Alabama State College. I taught thirty applied music students, organ and piano majors. I taught at a local high school and played at assemblies. I was playing for the church, had a family, and gave private piano lessons.

Reverend King had his father come and preach at Dexter. I recall the senior King preaching once about authentic things. The senior King said he did not want something as good as—he wanted the real thing.

One year Martin Luther King, Jr., invited the choir from his father's church in Atlanta to come and give a concert at Dexter. Dexter Avenue Baptist Church had a reputation for being a high church. I have never felt bad about that because there is nothing wrong with having cultivated minds in a congregation. Reverend King assured the body regarding the guests from Atlanta: "They know the type of music Dexter likes."

It was a very fine concert. The concert was tailored for Dexter. Dr. King's mother was the choir director. They sang a song entitled, "I Fall On My Knees and Cry Holy." My music teacher from the organ department at Alabama State College said that was the best selection rendered. The concert was to be an annual event, but it never took place again.

I have many fond recollections of Reverend King's pastorate at Dexter. His sermons were guides for living.

I remember Reverend King preaching a sermon on forgiveness. He said something came up and he offended someone in a mild way. Reverend King said the person offended told him: "I will forgive you, but not forget."

He preached on it and used this personal encounter as a practical illustration. Reverend King said:

"You must forget the pain and the quality that made it offensive. If you do not forget that, you have not forgiven."

On another Sunday he stood and before delivering his sermon he talked about people and their fear of flying. Someone in the membership must have mentioned his or her fear of flying to the pastor. Reverend King talked about the counter-productive dimension of fear. He pointed out that airplanes left Montgomery every day going to California. They landed safely. The safe landings never make the news because everything went well. The pilot was supposed to land the airplane safely. If an airplane falls out of the sky, that becomes news. You never hear on the news about the thousands of planes that land without any difficulty. You only hear about the few that crash.

I heard this illustration in the early 1960s. It has stayed with me.

In the summer of 1961, Wiley was awarded a National Science Foundation Scholarship to study at a summer institute for science teachers at Morgan State in Baltimore, Maryland. I went along for the ride. It turned out to be a very pleasant summer.

One of the high points of that trip was having the opportunity to attend an off-campus lecture. The subject was "Non-violent Social Change." The setting was a large Masonic Hall downtown. Martin Luther King, Jr., was the speaker.

Dr. King had risen to international prominence and his appearance in Baltimore drew a standing-room-only crowd. Wiley and I looked forward to the event. The days leading up to it were filled with anxiety. We became vicarious celebrities of sorts, as word spread over the campus that Dr. Martin Luther King, Jr., was our pastor.

On the day of the lecture, we were accompanied to the hall by a friend and fellow member of the summer institute who fancied himself a self-styled diplomat. For his own selfish reasons, he promised to wangle us through the crowd to exchange personal greetings with Dr. King. The individual fancying himself as a diplomat said that his picture participating in a lunch counter sit-in with his schoolmates in North Carolina had been published in newspapers and textbooks around the world. This, he contended, made him a bona fide member of the movement.

After what seemed to be about thirty minutes of scurrying through hallways, upstairs, around corners, etc., we were stopped by a guard who announced: "Reverend King is not seeing anyone before the lecture."

I took a piece of paper from my purse and penned a quick note: "Althea and Wiley Thomas from Dexter."

I handed it to the guard who took it in to my pastor. Moments later, Reverend King came out and greeted us warmly. We enjoyed a marvelous ninety-second reunion.

As always, Pastor King was never too busy for his members. He always had time for us.

My father studied at Hampton Institute. Upon learning that Dr. King had been assassinated, my father wrote a song entitled "Supplication." The words are:

> Give depth to our souls we pray
> Give love to our lives each day
> Give meaning to all we say.

It is a beautiful chant.

Mr. Wiley Thomas

I came to Montgomery in 1949 as a freshman at Alabama State College. About one year later I joined the United States Army. I was a soldier until 1953, when I was honorably discharged.

I returned to Montgomery and resumed my studies at Alabama State College. By May 1955 I had met all requirements for graduation. Dr. Martin Luther King, Jr., pastor of Dexter Avenue Baptist Church, was the baccalaureate speaker.

My wife, Althea, and I were brought up in the Methodist Church. Church has always been a very familiar place to me. My mother was very devout. If any of her children were slow on Sunday and did not attend worship service, that child or children had to go later and sit in the empty church for an hour anyway. Going to church has always been a part of my life.

Reverend King invited Althea to be the organist at Dexter Avenue Baptist Church in 1955. She accepted and we were present every Sunday. At that time we only had one car and were at Dexter each Sunday. After about a year, I said to Althea: "Let's join Dexter. You are there playing every Sunday. We might as well unite with this body of believers." So we did. That was in 1956.

As a boy, I was immersed in a creek. One has that option in the Methodist Church. My wife, however, was sprinkled as a girl. Reverend King said she had to be immersed. I often tease her about that.

Reverend King took great pains to preach excellent messages. He never entered the pulpit half cocked. Pastor King was always adequately prepared and preached a sound sermon. He was serious about his vocation and relationship with God. Reverend King communicated extremely well. He always had something relevant to say.

Reverend King was a pastor in the ultimate sense of the term. In my opinion, there is a huge difference between a pastor and a preacher. He was seriously involved with his flock and always engaged in everything at Dexter. As pastor, Reverend King was involved in all of the activities of the church. Our pastor knew every member of Dexter Avenue Baptist Church by name. That is one of the qualities of a pastor.

Some pastors will reprimand their congregations in a sermon. King would never go that route. That was one of his pastoral qualities. If your conscience did not reprimand you, it was not done.

Reverend King was a very sharp, immaculate dresser. He was not ostentatious, but well dressed at all times.

However, material things did not impress him. For example, the church had a red and white 1956 Chevy station wagon. Reverend King used to drive it around.

There was one thing in particular I appreciated about Reverend King as a pastor. He tried to change the lives of, and influence, those who did not go to church. Reverend King made every effort to identify with "the boys." He would go to the pool room where the "boys" hung out up around High and Jackson Streets. That element came to love Dr. King and had the utmost respect for him. That class bonded with him and he with them. Reverend King did not have a problem stopping to talk with fellows who were hanging out on the corner. He saw each person as a child of God.

I knew some of the guys who hung out in the vicinity of the pool room. One or two of them were real thugs. However these, too, loved Martin Luther King, Jr.

The world does not know it, but this class protected him. They would not let anything happen to Reverend King or allow anybody to bother him. They took care of King in their own way. Wherever he went the pool room element followed. This element usually will not follow preachers, but then preachers do not usually go to pool rooms either. Once one communicates genuinely with their class that person is one of them. They throw their arms around that person. Reverend King made them feel he cared about them and their condition, as a result they threw their arms around him.

For example, the night the parsonage was bombed it was not members from Dexter Avenue Baptist Church in Reverend King's front yard who were ready to erupt. Yes, some church members were present, but most of the people standing in the dark were community folk. The common people who loved and admired him.

Dexter Avenue Baptist Church had a reputation in the community. I think Reverend King was trying to help overcome the aloofness Dexter had in the community. He wanted to dispel the town myth about Dexter.

The movement started. I believe one of the reasons Reverend King got involved so quickly was because he was a true humanitarian. The issues that were being addressed were the types of concerns he was lifting up from the pulpit before everything kicked off. Before he became a public figure his preaching suggested that he was interested in humanitarian concerns, justice, and fairness for people.

It reached a point when the church was full every Sunday. Reverend King always had time for people. He was this way during his earliest years at Dexter and did not change once his prominence increased. At the height of the movement he still had time to stop and talk with parishioners and people in general.

I had a National Science Foundation Scholarship to study at Morgan State in Baltimore one summer in the early '60s. I met a man at Morgan State. His name was Muldrow. One day while reviewing a social studies book I found a picture of him on one of the pages. He and some other individuals were photographed sitting at a lunch counter in North Carolina. Aware of the fact that I was a member of Dexter Avenue Baptist Church, Muldrow said Dr. King was coming to Baltimore and he wanted to meet him. After Reverend King arrived in Baltimore, we found out where he was going to be speaking. Althea, Muldrow, a few others and I went to the location. We got someone to inform Reverend King that two of his Dexter members were present and wanted to say hello. Reverend King came out to greet us, as if to say, "Here are some of my children." It was as though I was bringing friends home. That is how Reverend King acted at all times.

Reverend King talked about equality, justice, and other similar themes. However, the one thing he often mentioned that sticks with me until this day was the "irreducible common denominator." People have differences, idiosyncrasies, attitudes, and such, but the irreducible common denominator, he used to say, was death. That makes us all equal.

I had no fear for Reverend King when the movement was in high gear. He seemed like he could come out of anything. I was shocked, therefore, beyond comprehension when he was killed. I am a true believer that the Lord knows best and everything happens for a reason.

As the old song goes in the Black church: "We will understand it better by and by."

Dr. Ralph Brison

I came to Montgomery in June 1953. I had just earned my Ph.D. at Ohio State. President Trenholm asked me to come to Alabama State College and teach summer school. I agreed expecting to go to another institution of higher learning to work in the fall. I received a very warm welcome at Alabama State and made many good friends during the summer.

Near the close of summer school President Trenholm called me to his office. He heard that I might be going to another institution to work. Dr. Trenholm was a fine, compassionate individual. Following my audience with him, I decided to remain at Alabama State.

I started attending Dexter Avenue Baptist Church that summer. My way to Dexter was well paved. I had a friend at Ohio State named Billy White. Billy's aunt, Mrs. Whitted, attended Dexter. Mrs. Whitted was also on the faculty at Alabama State College.

Reverend Vernon Johns was the pastor at that time. He was stirring things up even before Reverend King arrived. Johns would have us cringing in our seats. However, we admired him because he was wise and intelligent. Reverend Johns would rain down fire and brimstone on our heads.

Reverend Johns left Dexter to accept a position in Baltimore, Maryland. A number of ministers came to preach at Dexter during the interim.

One Sunday a young man named Martin King came to preach. His sermon was "Three D in Religion." During this time the three-dimension movies were popular, where viewers had to wear special glasses in order to see the movie perfectly and enjoy it. After hearing him, I said to myself—'That's it. This is the man.' The congregation loved his sermon. He was later called to be the pastor.

Reverend King was erudite and consistently challenging. His sermons were always uplifting and the kind that were good for us. Dexter was a middle-class congregation. The educational level of the members was such that we appreciated a well-developed, clearly thought-out sermon. He incorporated aspects of Black history. For example, he preached about the role of the Negro Spirituals. References were made to Frederick Douglass and the abolitionist movement. Martin was presaging events.

Martin appealed to us as a young man who had ideas and things he wanted to accomplish. Upon his arrival, Martin gave signs that he was full of ideas. He saw opportunities in this community that a young trained minister could seize. Martin had the qualifications and ability to carry out whatever vision he had. Long before December 1955 many in the church felt that Martin was special. It was apparent to many in the community, even before the bus boycott, that Martin was special.

When Martin was in the pulpit, we had to start putting chairs in the aisles. His reputation began to grow before the movement was in full gear.

Martin had charisma. He had the persona that went with a charismatic leader—warmth, intellect, compassion and understanding. These were the human qualities that endeared him to the people. We just loved the man.

Martin used to come to the Alabama State campus frequently. Robert Williams was on the music staff at the college. Robert and Martin were students at Morehouse College together. Martin would come to the campus to see Robert. Martin was an intellectual and a scholar. He enjoyed reading and visited the campus library frequently.

I knew Ralph Abernathy well. Ralph was a member of my fraternity—Kappa Alpha Psi. I was in close association with both preachers. Ralph and Martin were good for each other. Ralph did not have the intellectual quality that characterized Martin. This is not to demean Ralph. Martin's intellect was of the highest order. Ralph was a good follower. He could get things done and accepted that role. Martin needed such a person.

After the movement began, the members of Dexter Avenue Baptist Church naturally had to accept the fact that Martin would have to be shared. This was not a completely new position for us. We had to share him when he first arrived in Montgomery.

As Martin's fame spread, the congregation realized that he would not be able to preach to us each Sunday. We were satisfied with him preaching to us twice a month if it came to that. Of course, our preference was to have him with us every Sunday, but we were willing to live with a twice-monthly agreement.

When Martin's reputation became national, the members realized that we could not be demanding.

Martin's pastorate at Dexter was a golden age for us. This was a great time for the congregation. We had an excellent pastor, camaraderie, and a spirit of self-esteem. Our pastor was leading something that we all wanted to give vent to anyway. This filled us with much satisfaction.

It was a common scene to look out of the raised church windows on Sunday or leave church following the benediction and see the Klan gathered outside. By this time the Klan's impact had been curbed considerably. They did not strike fear in onlookers as in earlier years.

We adhered to Martin's wishes. If he asked for additional monies, several hundred dollars or whatever, for the movement, we gave it. He would say to us: "We here at Dexter have to lead the way."

Martin felt that the Dexter congregation had a special responsibility to the movement.

Dexter did have a special responsibility. There was a concentrated core of leaders in the congregation. For example, there was President Trenholm, Mrs. Jo Ann Robinson, Mrs. Burks, Mr. Richmond Smiley, and the Nesbitt family.

There was some fallout because of Martin's position and labors. Numerous instructors at Alabama State College, and members of Dexter Avenue Baptist Church, were terminated. Dr. Lawrence Reddick taught history at Alabama State College. He was one of the early historians of the movement and a close friend of Martin's. Governor Patterson instructed the college President to fire Dr. Reddick.

Many Dexter Avenue Baptist Church members were dismissed from places of employment. Those who worked at the college were not exempt. Dr. Trenholm called a meeting and expressed his regret about doing what he had been ordered to carry out. Mrs. Jo Ann Robinson was dismissed from the university as well as Mrs. Francis Burks. Both were members of Dexter. Several others of us anticipated getting our walking papers, but we survived.

The president was instructed to bar Martin from the campus. The latter could not visit his friends or keep up with his reading by using the library.

Mrs. Dorothy Posey

I became a member of Dexter Avenue Baptist Church when a little girl. I recall the young Reverend King. He was a wonderful, polite, and courteous person. He always tried to do right by everybody.

When in the pulpit, he kept the congregation awake. Listeners could not go to sleep on Reverend King. He kept everybody's attention. I had heard many ministers preach, but it was often difficult to follow those preachers. They would take a text and preach all around it. Those ministers would preach on a little of everything. It was common to just let your thoughts roam after listening for a few minutes. However, one's mind never drifted when Reverend King was preaching. A listener never lost his or her train of thought because Reverend King never abandoned his train of thought. One could follow everything he said and the sermon made sense from beginning to end. With many preachers one leaves church wondering, "What did he say?" Sometimes people ask themselves while the minister is preaching: "What is he trying to say or get across?" I always knew what Reverend King was saying. His sermons were clear and to the point. Each Sunday I left Dexter Avenue Baptist Church having something to carry into the coming week. It was easy to remember what Reverend King said.

Reverend King had an unlimited vocabulary. Once he started preaching the pastor would break those words down so that everybody in the congregation could understand the meaning. That was one of the ways he kept your attention.

Often Reverend King would tell a joke or incorporate a humorous story into his sermon. The anecdote or story always coincided with the sermon and helped bring alive the point he was trying to make. He told people how they should live.

I belonged to the Young Matrons Club of the church. Mrs. King was in charge of the group. We met each Tuesday night. The matrons gathered in a different home each week. Mrs. King was always present and enjoyed going to the various homes of church members. Sometimes I had other meetings on Tuesday evenings, but the Young Matrons was such an exciting club that I made it my business to be present.

One matter of business for the Matrons to discuss was what we were going to do in the church. We outlined how our club could support upcoming events at Dexter.

Reverend King was a sincere pastor. For example, when people could not get to worship service for lack of transportation he made arrangements for them to get to Dexter. The church had a station wagon. Reverend

King's position was that those who wanted to come to church and needed a ride should be accommodated.   A person was designated to drive the station wagon and transport those whose needs it met.

My husband, Eddie L. Posey, was a businessman. We owned a parking lot in the downtown area. We were the first local Black family to own a parking lot. People would park there for a day and pay a fee just as customers do at a downtown parking lot today. Most of our customers were white people. We had some Black customers, but most of our customers were white.

The bus boycott started. Black people in Montgomery did not ride the city bus for three hundred and eighty one days. Working persons had to get to their places of employment, but in support of the bus boycott did not ride public transportation. The Posey Parking Lot became a central meeting point. Eddie and I had been in possession of the lot for several years. Persons needing a ride to work came to the parking lot where rides were coordinated. Without the Posey Parking Lot I do not know where the people would have been picked up. It seemed like the most central location.

During the bus boycott, people left their churches and came to Dexter. Regular Dexter members could not even get to their usual seats on Sunday. We had to get there early to be seated. However, after the boycott ended, most seemed to have left Dexter. Attendance was low.

After the Selma to Montgomery March in 1965, I noticed a sudden change in the patronage of our white customers. The white motorists stopped using the Posey Parking Lot completely.

Black people did not support us as they should have. Eddie and I had to give the lot up. This took us by surprise. We never envisioned this loss when events took off in Montgomery. Eddie and I had three children whom we loved and had to take care. The Posey family depended on that parking lot.

Even though we lost our business we still supported Reverend King. We did not withdraw from Reverend King in spite of our personal pain. We felt that what he was doing was right, just, and fair. Eddie and I decided that we would not become angry or bitter, but would pray our way through it. That is exactly what we did.

Numerous Black businesses have gone out of existence since integration.

With the assassination of Reverend King we lost a great leader. However, we cannot look back. We have to keep going forward and looking ahead. Looking and going forward are a must so that we can do better things, so Black people can love one another, work together, and help each other.

Mrs. Claressa W. Chambliss

When Reverend King came to Dexter Avenue Baptist Church to preach initially, I listened to him. He was good. He was a fantastic preacher. However, I said to myself—"He is too young for Dexter." Reverend King had not completed his Ph.D. program at Boston University and was still traveling back and forth. "We just do not need a pastor that young," I thought. However, after listening to his preaching for some time, it got to the point where I did not want to go to worship service if someone was preaching other than the young Reverend King.

After Reverend and Mrs. King moved into the parsonage, the Women's Council of the church gave a food shower for the young pastor and his lovely bride. We carried different types of food to them. Both were appreciative and expressed their thanks.

We later learned of our young pastor's love for rich home-cooked foods. One of his favorite desserts was pound cake. Mrs. Doak and I used to bake them for him. He said once: "I like pound cake hot just as it comes out of the oven."

At first I thought he was too young and not ready for Dexter Avenue Baptist Church; but after Reverend King had been with us for a while I found that Dexter was not ready for him. The things Reverend King would do and say made my concern for his youth dissipate. After a little while, he was just a fine young man in my book. He was the kind of person you were never afraid to be around.

He was a pastor to all the people. His home was open to parishioners. I recall stopping by twice to visit.

Shortly after Reverend King's arrival the Rosa Parks incident occurred. Some of the prime movers behind the Montgomery Bus Boycott were some women who belonged to Dexter Avenue Baptist Church. I was a cosmetologist. Jo Ann Robinson, Mary Francis Burks, Bernice Andrews, and some other women got their hair fixed at my establishment. They were my clients. The three ladies named were making arrangements and talking about the bus boycott in the beauty shop and outlining a strategy one day. Jo Ann, now deceased, wrote a book entitled *The Women Behind the Montgomery Bus Boycott*. Much of what she, Mary Francis, and Bernice did can be found in Jo Ann's publication.

My husband, Osborne, went to the first mass meeting at. Upon returning home that night, he said to me: "Your pastor was elected to head the bus boycott."

Osborne said "your pastor" because he was not a member of Dexter at the time. He joined later. That Reverend King had been elected to head the bus boycott movement surprised me. I had not completely gotten over the dominating presence of his youth. However, Reverend King had done such a marvelous job re-organizing the church, establishing various clubs, and such, that I felt he could handle the leadership position in the bus boycott. He was young, but it did not take long to figure out that he was the right man for the task.

It reached the point where my husband and I would hardly ever miss a mass meeting. We had to leave home about 4:30 p.m. or 5:00 p.m. in order to get a seat.

Those persons boycotting the bus system needed rides to and from work. I used to get up and be at First Baptist Church at 4:30 a.m. I drove people to work until 7:00 a.m. I was in class at 8:00 a.m. at Alabama State College. My classes were from 8:00 a.m. to 12:00. Dr. Trenholm allowed me to arrange my schedule that way. He was deeply concerned about the students and did everything within his power to assist them. At 12:00 noon I opened up my business. I would work in my shop until 10:00 p.m. or 11:00 p.m. At 4:30 a.m. the following morning I was back at First Baptist transporting riders.

The MIA provided gas to drivers. My husband and I never accepted any gas. We believed in the cause and put gas in our vehicles ourselves.

One local historical event that is seldom lifted up that happened during the bus boycott was the number of white people who supported the cause. Many whites in Montgomery believed that Black people were justified in their actions. White advocates did not support us openly. They feared reprisal from the larger white community. However, many local whites sent monies to the mass meetings. Some white families sent donations regularly by their maids who put the contributions in the collection plates at the mass meetings. The bus boycott had been in progress for some time before monies to support it really started flowing in from outside Montgomery and outside of the State of Alabama. Local monies undergirded the work initially. Local Black and white people were donating.

I remember one occasion when Reverend King was arrested. A trial date was set. Black people were supposed to walk to his trial. That is exactly what happened. Nobody drove that day. All walked to the courthouse. There were so many people present that it was impossible to get in. My husband was a letter carrier and knew of another entrance near the judge's chambers. Osborne got in.

A sheriff said to us who had difficulty getting in: "Don't you all know this building is condemned? It is going to fall down and kill you."

"If the building falls, it will kill you too," I pointed out. He went silent.

Reverend King was a marvelous leader. One night we had a meeting at First Baptist Church, where Reverend Ralph Abernathy was the pastor. Before leaving home I told my husband I wanted to go back in the house and get my house shoes.

"I might need them," I said.

While we were in the meeting at First Baptist, white people were going around the church setting on fire the vehicles of those inside. Along with that episode they tossed tear gas in the church. The people inside panicked. I suppose the tear gas was intended to drive us out of the church into the streets where opponents waited.

"Just be calm," Reverend King urged.

Reverend King went downstairs and telephoned the United States Attorney General, Robert Kennedy.

The Attorney General said: "I will inform the President."

President Kennedy called Governor Patterson and instructed him to put out the National Guard. When the National Guard came out, Robert Kennedy federalized them. Once federalized the National Guard came under the authority of the Federal Government.

The telephone calls and negotiating went on throughout the evening. We stayed in the church all night. Reverend King stayed with us.

It was sunup before we went out. Reverend King announced to us the following morning: "The National Guard has been federalized. They will see to it that all of you get home safe."

We were at First Baptist Church on another night. Reverend King and several other ministers were in the pulpit. Reverend King had an unusual look on his face. I noticed it immediately. The program was proceeding. However, I knew something was not right. I leaned over in the pew and whispered to Osborne: "Something is wrong."

We later learned that the parsonage had been bombed. Like hundreds of others in the city we rushed to the parsonage. When my husband and I arrived, hundreds of people were in the front yard. Mayor Gayle was there and other city officials. Policemen were there waving their nightsticks and instructing people to move on and return home. A policeman told me to move and leave the premise.

"This is our property," I said. "This is the church's parsonage. I can stand here."

Mayor Gayle came out on the porch to talk to the people in the yard. He was booed by the crowd. The mayor raised his hands to get our attention. The more he tried to get the attention of the people in the yard the more they hissed him.

Reverend King came out onto the porch. The hissing and booing ceased. He said that everyone in the house was fine.

"Go home and get a good night's rest," he urged.

The crowd in the front yard responded like a flock of sheep. Each turned and headed home as instructed.

Reverend King was a true pastor. It reached the point where his opponents were out to kill him. We all knew that. When I was in the hospital at Saint Margaret's he came to see me.

I said to him: "You should not be out."

I appreciated his pastoral visit, but I feared for his safety. In fact, I feared for his life.

"I just came across the street," he said.

I felt he had no business being visible and walking across the street. However, Reverend King felt he had to carry out his pastoral duties which included visiting members in the hospital. He was busy during this time, but not too busy to neglect his pastoral duties.

Reverend King did many wonderful acts and accomplished much. However, as an individual and parishioner, my most memorable and touching experience was his visit to the hospital to visit me when I was ill. He came to see a member of the flock even though his own life was in immediate danger. I do not know who drove him there that night. I was probably more fearful about my pastor's life than was he about his own life. Reverend King put my care above the care of his own life that evening.

There was a serious move on to destroy Reverend King. A prominent Black family took Reverend and Mrs. King into their home on one occasion for a few days. I will intentionally withhold the identification of the family. Osborne and I learned that Reverend and Mrs. King were there. We went out and purchased a ham. I baked it and laced it with all the trimmings. We later made arrangements to drop the ham off to Pastor King. I felt that doing something nice like that would have cheered him up. Reverend King always enjoyed good home-cooked food.

When he was stabbed by the woman in New York, all of us were moved. Everybody was praying day and night.

Whenever something came up with Reverend King, we became concerned and prayed. We had to do a lot of praying back then. Prayer kept fear away. One time he got the hiccups. It would not cease. Reverend King had it for about a week. All we could do was pray.

Around 1959 I began to notice a change in my pastor. Many of his followers and supporters were withdrawing. I could tell from his sermons he was a little disgusted and hurt. He was being so brave and his followers were getting weak. People started coming forward as if they wanted to be a leader. There was a definite turn in Reverend King's disposition. One could hear it in his sermons and speeches.

Reverend King resigned from Dexter Avenue Baptist Church and left the city of Montgomery. I wanted him to leave. I admired Reverend King and supported him, but I did not want to see the young man I had watch mature get hurt. For example, when he was stabbed by the woman in New York, a Black man in our community said: "I am sorry and glad."

Some of my clients were talking about the man's statement one day.

I was also afraid for Reverend King regarding his inner circle. I had reservations about one or two persons close to him. People will do anything for power and those closest to you can do the most harm.

Reverend King was a wonderful leader and a dynamic individual. He enjoyed unparalleled success. However, Reverend Vernon Johns laid the foundation.

Reverend Johns was trying to arouse Black people in the community from their slumber, during his period of ministry. For example, a white merchant owned a business on the corner of Union and Terrell Streets. He raped a Black girl who was baby-sitting for him. Reverend Johns tried to get the Black community to respond. The people would not follow him.

The difficulty with Reverend Johns was his leadership style. He was not patient like Reverend King. Reverend Johns wanted results and he wanted them at that moment.

Reverend King was patient. That was one of his noble qualities. That quality, his patience, proved to be one of the prize elements in the struggle.

Osborne and I continued to follow Reverend King via television news after he left Montgomery. It seemed like the farther he got away from us the closer he got. One evening we were watching television and something was said about Reverend King and the Far East. I said to my husband: "I don't want Reverend King in politics. It's too dirty for him."

The Selma to Montgomery March was held in 1965. This event brought Reverend King back to Alabama. When the Selma to Montgomery March was held, we had two young ministers from Pennsylvania staying in our home. One was Black and the other white. The march began a few days earlier and the marchers were nearing Montgomery. The two preachers wanted to meet the marchers along the route and participate by marching into Montgomery with them. I took them one morning to where some MIA members were to depart and go meet the marchers. When I arrived with the two young clergymen, the MIA people had already departed. I then drove down the Selma Highway in the direction from which the marchers were coming. My plan was to let the two ministers out so they could join up when the marchers drew near; and I would return to Montgomery. However, the State Highway Patrol would not allow me to stop and put them out. Each time I stopped to let the pair out a patrolman would urge me to move on. Well, after a while, I stopped and told the two they should get out. I let the preachers out on the road and turned around to head back to Montgomery.

The State Highway Patrol began to pursue me. I accelerated to a high rate of speed. I was young then and could do that. I began to outdistance the patrol car.

Reverend King and some of the leading ministers were participating in the march. The clergy were supposed to assemble at Dexter Avenue Baptist Church after returning to Montgomery. Some of the ladies of the church were responsible for providing a reception for the ministers. It was my task to cook some stringbeans. I had my pot of stringbeans in the car as I was escaping the patrolman. Reverend King loved stringbeans and my only prayer was: "Lord, don't let this pot of stringbeans turn over."

The patrolman turned around. I thought to myself that he probably recorded my license plate number and would later seek an arrest. The car was registered in my husband's name. I became concerned for Osborne.

I reached Decatur Street which is the street next to Dexter Avenue Baptist Church. A white lady said to me: "You better not park there."

"Why not?"

"If you park there, your car might be burned up when you come back." she warned.

"Burn it," I said. "The insurance company will pay."

I went into the church and we began to prepare for the reception of Reverend King and his entourage.

I never met a young man as determined as was Reverend King. I think God put him in Montgomery to execute the grand work in this city with which his name will be eternally associated.

Mr. Osborne C. Chambliss

A friend of mine, Willie Williams, and his wife were at our house the night the first mass meeting was to be held. Willie and I decided to go. What a sight caught our eyes when we neared Holt Street Baptist Church. A large crowd of people was visible. There was no parking within close proximity of the church. We had to park eight or ten blocks away and walk back to the church. We managed to get inside.

It was a moving evening. A collection was taken to help establish a fund to advance the cause. I wore a gray hat that evening. My hat was used to collect money. I clearly remember that gray hat being full of money that night after it had been passed around. Other hats were also used and were equally full.

The gathering at Holt Street Baptist Church was the greatest thing to happen in this city as far as I am concerned and was one of the most memorable events of the bus boycott era. To see so many Black people, formerly fragmented and divided, rally like we did that evening was thrilling.

Willie and I left the church. Both of us were excited. On the way back to my house I asked: "Willie, what do you think about the great meeting we just left?"

With excitement in his voice, Willie replied: "Man, you know this is something to see. The people coming together like this. We have a wonderful leader. I don't believe the white folk can get to him."

We entered my house and told all that had taken place.

The bus boycott started. Initially Black people walked. On the Monday the boycott started there had been no coordination of rides for workers. It was only supposed to last one day. The Monday event was extremely successful. People walked to work or got to their places of employment the best way they could. At the Monday night meeting at Holt Street Baptist Church it was decided that the boycott would continue.

On Tuesday morning individuals with automobiles started picking up other persons and taking them to their destinations. A serious well-thought-out program was implemented to provide rides for those workers who supported the bus boycott.

Reverend King was a different type of leader. Local white people had always been able to get to our Black leaders. We would start a program or some effort designed to strengthen ourselves and ultimately challenge the unfair local oppressive system, the program would work for a short period of time, then fade out of existence. Our hopes had been lifted and lowered on several previous occasions. Whoever the Black leaders were prior to

Reverend King, they would be given money under the table or made promises that would benefit them and not Black people as a whole. The money and or promises were always sufficient to get the individuals to forget about the people and surrender. The hopes of the Black community were dashed to the ground a number of times.

It seemed like things were going to be different with Reverend King. The white establishment had not changed. The white establishment undoubtedly desired to get to Reverend King, but was unable to make inroads with him for two reasons. First, events took off so fast and the Black community united so rapidly until there was no time for them to approach Reverend King. Secondly, Reverend King was still relatively new in town and for this reason the establishment could not get to him as quickly as desired.

An old Black lady told Reverend King one evening at a meeting: "Reverend King, you got us cemented together. You got us cemented together."

She was right. That was a main ingredient to the success of the bus boycott—Reverend King had us cemented together.

Reverend King was once summoned by city authorities and influential persons in Montgomery. They offered him money to surrender, but he declined. Many other local Black leaders had been given monies in the past. White people thought it would work this time. They were mistaken. This standard operating procedure did not work with Reverend King. He was more than just the head of something, Reverend King was committed to that which he was leading. The establishment could not get to Reverend King. They tried repeatedly, but they could not buy him. Reverend King's stand inspired his followers.

Reverend King was arrested on one occasion. It was agreed that the Black people in Montgomery would not drive that day, but would walk to the trial.

There were so many people at the courthouse until it was impossible to get inside when Claressa and I arrived. As a letter carrier, I was familiar with all of the various entrances of local buildings. I knew of an entrance near the judge's chamber. I entered there.

The trial was something to behold. The courtroom was filled to capacity. The seating was segregated. All of the white people were seated on one side and all of the Black people on the other side. The African Methodist Episcopal Zion Church had several of their top lawyers from around the country to come to Montgomery. There was one African Methodist Episcopal Zion lawyer seated on the Black side of the courtroom. He was instructed to move to the side where all of the whites were sitting.

"I am a Black man," he said to the surprise of the courtroom authorities.

The attorney was one of the AMEZ lawyers and could have very easily passed for a white person. The attorney remained on the side of the courtroom with his race.

It seemed as if the authorities could not decide with what to charge Reverend King. After the court session, we went to Dexter Avenue Baptist Church and thanked God for the victory heaven secured for Reverend King. Reverend B. D. Lambert, pastor of Maggie Street Baptist Church, led the prayer. Oh my, could he pray. Nobody could pray like Reverend Lambert and Reverend King admired him. I only remember one part of Reverend Lambert's prayer: "Lord, we just thank You. You just confused the white folks today. They did not know what to do."

The establishment was unable to get to Reverend King. Neither threats, offers of money, attacks, promises, nor anything was suitable to get him to veer from his commitment. The Black people of the community had put their full confidence in Reverend King.

Since those in power could not turn Reverend King around, they tried to turn those of us in his corner against him. All types of ruses were employed. For example, I got a telephone call one day from someone at the city jail. I was told by a King supporter that the authorities had a list of local Black people who were to be arrested. My name, I was informed, was on the list. My wife and I went to the jailhouse. Claressa volunteered to be arrested. However, she was not put under arrest. Claressa was a self-employed cosmetologist. Arresting her or making sure she had a criminal record would not have hurt her business in any way. Most of her customers were supporters of Reverend King.

I was put under arrest, fingerprinted, and charged as a criminal. My crime was supporting Reverend King and the movement. My case was different from my wife's. I was a mail carrier—a Federal employee. Acquiring a criminal record was supposed to be more costly for me. Whatever their design it did not work. Numerous Black people were at the jailhouse that day and left having criminal records.

The ploy was very unorganized. For example, I was charged and put under arrest. I had to make bail. A Black man who had already been charged and arrested signed for my release. I turned around and signed for his bail. Now how can two men under arrest sign for each other's release?

The aim was obvious. Some whites thought that if they made it costly enough for those of us who were working persons in certain career fields we would desert Reverend King. If anything, their actions made King supporters more determined.

Opponents of Reverend King wanted him dead. Some of the men who admired and appreciated the dedication of Reverend King took it upon themselves to provide protection for him.

I used to stand guard at the parsonage on Wednesday night. I kept a weapon with me. After some time, Reverend King discovered I carried a gun when standing guard. He said to me in a nice pastoral manner: "Brother Osborne, I am non-violent. This protest is non-violent in nature. You will have to put your weapon away."

I explained that I did not fully embrace the philosophy of non-violence. Reverend King did not grow angry. He understood that many Black people had a difficult time embracing the idea of non-violence in the face of what we as a people were experiencing.

A national news company came to interview Reverend King. The interview was short-circuited and could not be seen on local television. Some of us went down to the church where the interview was being conducted. Klansmen were all around Dexter Avenue Baptist Church. A young white man said something to me and I replied: "You are dealing with the wrong fellow now. Reverend King is non-violent. I am not Reverend King."

I admired Reverend King and his position. I did not want to be separated from him or withdraw my support. The work he had undertaken was too important. The cause headed by him was meaningful to me and I wanted to contribute. I voluntarily relinquished my services as a guard at the parsonage.

However, another work immediately awaited my hands. I took on the responsibility of riding in the back-up car behind Reverend King. Mr. Cleveland Dennard, who later became President of Atlanta University, and I rode in the second car. Since threats were being made on Reverend King's life, we always had two or three cars available for him. The enemy never knew which car he was riding in. Reverend King would be driven to a church or speaking engagement in one car and leave in another.

The people were committed to seeing this event through to the end at all cost. The lives of the men who protected Reverend King were in danger also, but as the old lady said that night at the meeting—Reverend King had us cemented together.

While I considered it a privilege to ride in the second car and protect Reverend King, I was always nervous. Each time we went out drivers and back-up drivers were nervous. However, those of us who had our minds made up did not care. Like our leader Reverend King, we wanted to see this thing through to the end.

I can recount an incident when our nervousness was brought to a head. One night Reverend King was to make a speech at a local CME Church on

Glass Street. He was inside the church. The people were singing and praying. As was the case when Reverend King was scheduled to speak, the church was full. The other person and I in the second car waited outside in the vehicle. It was dark. Suddenly a loud noise engulfed us. It was not the sound of people singing. The two of us in the back-up car did not know what to think. Our hearts raced. Both of us almost jumped out of the car. We had no idea what was going on. Finally we figured it out. The sound that suddenly filled the night air were sirens from fire trucks.

This too was a ploy. There was no fire at the church. Opponents pretended the church was ablaze. Upon hearing the sirens and learning about fire trucks coming to the church, those inside were supposed to panic, rush out of the church, and stampede each other while fleeing to safety, thus causing the meeting to come to an end. However, the plan did not work. The people in the church kept right on singing and praying. My wife was inside.

Through it all Reverend King remained jovial. He loved to joke and had a grand sense of humor.

He was a great leader, but even more so an excellent pastor. Reverend King went wherever there were people. He would walk into the poolroom as well as the night club and talk to people. These are places where a preacher would not dare go. The people would talk to him. Reverend King would go to the Citizens Club, a night club on the corner of Myles and Charlotte Streets. He would tell the people what was expected of them. In pool rooms the men stopped whatever they were doing and listened to him.

Reverend King would walk down Monroe Street here in Montgomery and talk to every wino. All of them would stop and listen to him. He could dialogue with all people.

Above all I enjoyed the Holy Communion Service conducted by Reverend King. It was a most impressive event. It was held at night on the first Sunday in the month. The lights would be turned out. Only the lighted cross in the background hanging over the pulpit area from the ceiling was visible. Reverend King would sit behind the table, following the pattern we see of Jesus in pictures sitting at the table with His disciples. Then Reverend King would say: "He sat down with the twelve...."

Many Black domestic workers lost their jobs during the movement, but practically all of them secured employment elsewhere immediately. They did not earn much, but worked very hard. As long as the struggle was advancing and the Black domestics and common people were losing their jobs, Reverend King had the support of almost all of the Black community. However, when his labors and mission began to affect the livelihood and security of another element among the local Black population, this class asserted that Reverend King had overstepped his bounds.

When this element of Black people began to move aside so the strong wind could blow against Reverend King only, he realized what was happening. He was in his automobile at Winston Craig's gas station one day. I happened to be at the gas station also. Reverend King said to me, while sitting in his car: "Brother Osborne, I am going to leave Montgomery." Reverend King was somewhat dejected. "Many of the people I thought were with me are against me."

I think the people who were now against him shocked Reverend King beyond description. It was a severe blow. Moreover, the blow came from the people he least expected to turn on him. Reverend King did not say he was departing Montgomery immediately. However, it was apparent that he saw what was happening.

The conversation I had with Reverend King at the gas station that day was one of the most moving episodes for me during the King era in Montgomery. He did not share this with many people right away. I am not sure why he told me, but I count it a blessing that he thought enough of Osborne C. Chambliss to have shared such a deep inward personal feeling.

A bi-racial committee composed of city residents was formed. Mr. Winston Craig, a member of Dexter and worker at the governor's mansion, was instrumental in getting this committee together. The committee consisted of forty-five whites and forty-five Black people. The Black people had a chairman and so did the white people, with one person over the whole committee. The bi-racial committee's task was to work with city officials and the mayor in order to keep calm in Montgomery.

The 1965 Selma to Montgomery March was being planned. A meeting was held at the Chamber of Commerce. Upon arriving, we discovered that a newspaper was available with the names of the forty-five Black committee members. The paper claimed that the Black members were opposed to the Selma to Montgomery March. That was not true. This was another attempt to weaken Reverend King's base of support even though he no longer lived in Montgomery. Most favored the idea. However, to the surprise of many in the meeting several Black people did stand up and say: "We are opposed to the Selma to Montgomery March."

Many of the Black members were stunned. The thing that shocked and hurt the most were the persons who made the announcement. They were individuals who had been strong supporters of Reverend King during his years in Montgomery and in his company frequently. The establishment had gotten to them. Some people were now in it for whatever they could gain for themselves.

Those opposed to the Selma to Montgomery March consisted of another class of Black people.

These were people who basically had good jobs, homes, and security. However, it appeared that they were not secure enough to take a stand for humanity.

Mr. David Ross

My grandfather founded the funeral home of which I am the current president. Today it is known as Ross-Clayton Funeral Home, Montgomery, Alabama. I was born in 1948. My parents were educated. Black boys and girls of educated parents in the South during the 1940s and 1950s were shielded from the overt harshness of the insensitive racist environment in which they were growing up. However, there came a time for all Black youngsters to face the realities of the day. Facing the realities meant directly encountering racial indignities or being an eyewitness to some Black adult suffering some unpleasantness from white people.

My first encounter with the harsh realities of the South occurred when I was about six years old. My mother had a cousin who lived on Early Street here in Montgomery. We rode the city bus one day to see my mother's cousin. The city bus line ended in that vicinity and usually turned around at the end of Early Street. My mother and I were still on the bus when the driver turned around and started back in the opposite direction. The only other person on the bus was a young Black domestic who appeared to be in her early twenties.

The driver said to my mother: "You better get up here and put another fare in the box."

The young Black female began to mumble something about white people. My mother deposited the fare and returned to her seat. She began to speak softly.

"If you don't hush, I am going to put you off of this bus," the driver told mother.

"No, you won't," she replied emphatically.

The driver hushed and continued his route. He quickly realized this was a different type of woman. Though a boy, I sensed that day my mother meant business and would have harmed the driver had the need arisen. This was before Black people took it upon themselves to articulate their views and feelings to white folk in a public setting. I could tell my mother was ready to die that day.

Shortly after that incident Reverend King was called to be the pastor of Dexter Avenue Baptist Church. As a boy of six years of age, I recall how small in physical stature our new pastor seemed. He was not a large man. I knew some teenage boys who were as large as the pastor. Looking back I realize how right I was. Reverend King was very small when he arrived.

Dexter was a status quo church. The membership was small. You could get a seat on any Sunday. I remember Reverend King preaching. He was a blistering orator. Words rolled from his lips like rain. After his arrival, the increase in attendance was obvious even to a child.

Shortly after Reverend King arrived the bus boycott started. I did not have a clear vision of what was going on in 1955 and 1956. Nevertheless, as a boy I could tell something unusual, different, and radical was happening. You could feel it in the air. Any thinking child over six or seven knew that something big was happening in Montgomery. Black people were acting different. It was as if something had come over the members of my race. As a boy, I knew something was happening that was going to change my life and condition. I knew it was going to change the lives of all Black people. It reached the point at church on Sunday that the sanctuary overflowed and people were in the lower level of the church listening to Reverend King. It was these signs that clued the children in that something big was taking place in Montgomery.

I continued to develop in age and reason for myself. Children did not have a lot of direct contact with adults. The latter kept company among themselves. Boys and girls often had to draw their own conclusions about matters. I did so regarding my pastor. I could tell that Reverend King was real. He was not grandstanding. As a lad, I realized that Reverend King was different. I did not see men like him everyday. It appeared that he saw a bigger picture and had a higher calling. He was no average man in the neighborhood. You just knew he was special. It was like looking down through the pages of history. We children would stare at him in respect. He never let any of us down. To the children who had faced indignities and watched adult relatives and friends endure the same, Reverend King was to us a super man. He was our hero. The boys and girls truly looked up to the little preacher who was trying to make a big difference.

Reverend King's sermons were relevant even to a boy of my age. I can recall many of his words. I remember hearing countless sermons on forgiving. "Remember the Bible," he used to say. I have the utmost respect for God's word to this day. When the number of participants in the movement had swollen, some Black people wanted to get violent. Reverend King said no. I recall his reminder that there were some good white people and we could not become violent. He was a voice for the decent white people.

By the time I was twelve or thereabouts I had had several brushes with the evil force known as racism. I felt that pain in the worst way because I had come from a sheltered situation. I was crushed deeply on several occasions. What Black people had to encounter back then was almost impossible to resist. Black adults had to endure the same type of indignities that children suffered. The status of Black adults did not protect them. Teachers, preachers, and the non-professionals were exposed to the same harsh insults.

Life for Black people in Montgomery was horrible in the 1950s. There were men like Mr. E. D. Nixon and Mr. Rufus Lewis who labored for the advancement of the race. Reverend King helped the people in our town get a taste of dignity. Once they got that taste it was impossible for anyone to remove it. I got the feeling, as a boy, that Black people were literally ready to die to secure full dignity. They had had enough. They sensed the Lord had sent them a leader.

This leader was fearless. There is fear in all people. It usually manifests itself when one confronts a system such as the one that existed in Montgomery in the 1950s. Reverend King showed no fear. It was as though he had complete confidence in God. This fearlessness on Reverend King's part impressed me greatly as a boy. I knew the situation and condition of Black people were going to change. The only surprise was how fast it changed. I thought the movement Reverend King was leading would go on for a long long time before matters were resolved.

While all the activity was going on in Montgomery, Dexter Avenue Baptist Church continued to function as a local Baptist congregation. There was Sunday afternoon Baptist Training Union (BTU). I attended Vacation Bible School during the summer. There was a group for youth called The Sunbeamers. Mrs. Lame Davis headed this group. Mrs. Davis would not let up on the youth. There was a group for boys known as the Crusaders. With the Crusaders the adult leaders attempted to relate Christian principles to everyday life. At the Sunday meetings God and the Bible were discussed. The boys were expected to employ these principles at school during the week. We were taught weekly to do right. We were also taught to be sympathetic, to respect older people, honor the preacher and his wife, etc.

It was also emphasized in the Crusaders that every person should get a good education. This idea was pushed unendingly. It was explained to us that education was one of the main routes to success. That stuck with me. I remember education being one of Reverend King's themes.

When I was about twelve years old, my mother pulled me aside one day. She said: "David, it is time for you to be baptized." The decision was completely mine, but I agreed with her. It was time for me to get baptized. My mother went on to say: "I want Reverend King to baptize you. This is important to me. Reverend King is going to be famous." Looking to the future and at me, she added: "And he is going to be in history books one day."

My mother envisioned the joy and pride I would have in manhood being able to say—"I was baptized by Reverend Martin Luther King, Jr."

Shortly after our conversation I walked down the aisle one Sunday following Reverend King's sermon. I remember standing in front of the congregation. The little giant, Reverend King, put his arm around my shoulder and said to the audience something along this line: "This boy is giving his life to Christ today. This is the greatest day of his life and the wisest decision he will ever make."

I remember the Sunday I was baptized. Reverend King had become a prominent figure. He was a preacher of the Gospel. He was living the type of life that, according to Sunday School and Vacation Bible School lessons, one should live. He was working to make life richer for people who were being taken advantage of and telling bad men they should repent and treat everybody right. To the mind of a boy, being baptized by Reverend King was almost like being baptized by Jesus. I knew Reverend King was a man, a human being just as I was, but considering who he was and the impact he was making I knew that the hands of a rare individual were lowering me into the water.

Deacon Richard Jordan

My family's roots are deep in the church known today as Dexter Avenue King Memorial Baptist Church. I joined Dexter Avenue Baptist when a youngster. The church was without a pastor around 1954. A young minister named Martin King came to preach. He was a candidate for the pulpit. After preaching his first sermon, Reverend King became the leading contender for the pulpit.

I was a sophomore at Alabama State College when Reverend King came to deliver his sermons as a candidate. I was impressed with his stature, immaculate dress, his sermon delivery, and articulation. That he was highly educated was very apparent. He was knowledgeable in philosophy. This young minister was philosophical in his sermons. That impressed me greatly. One reason I was so moved was because I was taking philosophy at school that year. Reverend King was using terms and articulating concepts that I had already learned or was learning. It was the wish of the college students in the church that Reverend King would be called to be the pastor.

Our prayers were answered. Reverend King was called by the congregation to pastor the church.

Reverend King's father, affectionately known as Daddy King, was the guest preacher at his son's installation service. The senior King loved his son and was greatly concerned about how the young King would be treated at his first charge. King, Jr., came from a fine background. His parents were educated. It was apparent that the King family of Atlanta was not beholden to anyone, nor was King, Jr. I remember Daddy King saying to the congregation: "I have heard about you folk at Dexter. You do not like to keep a preacher long." Daddy King was clear as to how he expected his son to be treated among us. He went on to say: "My son is used to nice clothes, a nice car, and having money in his pocket. Don't mistreat him! If you want to mistreat him, send my son back to Ebenezer."

This charge gave King, Jr., added authority to come in and do some restructuring at Dexter Avenue Baptist Church. Reverend King organized the Month Clubs and several other clubs, consolidated the budget, formed the Voter Registration Committee, Board of Christian Education, and a church paper, *The Echo Newspaper.* A host of ladies' and men's auxiliaries came into being. The Young Matrons were revitalized. These women were around the age of Reverend King's wife, Coretta, who headed this group. She and my wife, Viola, car-pooled to the matrons' meetings.

Reverend King's trained theological background made him a local attraction. The professors and students from the campus started coming to

Dexter Avenue Baptist Church. Dr. King had that special something that drew people. Individuals began to gravitate to him long before any organized civil activities started in Montgomery.

Dr. King's sermons were very moving and I can remember many that were preached when I was a college student. I had a very rare opportunity as a student and member of Dexter. A friend of mine, Alfred Young, and I used to go to the parsonage on Sunday afternoons. The morning sermon was played back on a tape recorder. Reverend King would expound more in detail for us.

Later we discovered that Dr. King was an Alpha man. The brothers of Alpha Phi Alpha Fraternity, Inc., on the campus learned about the Sunday afternoon gathering at the parsonage and started attending. When Sunday afternoon was inconvenient, an evening during the week was chosen and we met with Reverend King at that time.

Dr. King was more interesting in the Sunday afternoon setting. We could engage him. It was like being in a class, but richer. The Alpha brothers came to hear their sagacious brother talk philosophy. We had our own Sunday afternoon academy on Jackson Street where the parsonage was located. Dr. King was extremely delighted with these sessions. He was taken with the students and their interest.

The Sunday afternoon sessions started out as philosophical dialogues. Many of the Alpha Phi Alpha brothers who attended these sessions and listened to sermons at Dexter ascended to great heights. John Porter, T. Y. Rogers, Harold Carter, James Carter and another brother, last name Watson, became preachers. I cannot recall Brother Watson's first name. There is no doubt that Dr. King had an impact on each of the five named.

There was a student named Grady Anderson who attended the Sunday afternoon study sessions. He became an officer in his church and served in this capacity for many years. In later life Anderson answered the call to the Christian ministry. He is now a minister. Reverend King influenced him also.

Dr. King was fond of his fraternity. He started attending frat meetings.

Many of the undergraduate frat brothers were devilish. We used to have Saturday night parties. I was one of the main instigators. Once the brothers decided to have a picnic on some unknown white man's land in Montgomery County. That should have been unfashionable because the Civil Rights Movement was in progress. The brothers laid their things out on the green grass that warm day planning to just relax, kick back, and have some fun.

The white owner approached us and inquired: "Who gave you all permission to stop here and use this property?"

"No one," we confessed and explained further, "we are students at Alabama State College. We planned a picnic and decided this nice green spot would be ideal."

To our surprise the man said we could stay.

"Just clean the place up before you leave," he demanded.

That was not asking much and the brothers assured him we would honor his request. We laid out our refreshments, reclined on the grass, and began to enjoy ourselves. About ten minutes after getting situated we saw a car rolling up. We were stunned to see Reverend King. We were glad to see him on the one hand, but on the other the brothers were somewhat embarrassed. We had some spirits. His presence was unexpected. The fraternity brothers did not know what to say, but we knew what to do. All began to scramble looking for places to hide our delights. Nobody was going to be bold enough to display them before Reverend King. All had the utmost respect for him. Events happened so rapidly that we were not able to conceal all of the beverages.

He parked, got out of the car and came over to where we were. To our surprise he said: "Bring me one."

We knew what he meant. Somebody gave him a can of beverage. Reverend King held it up toward the sky, and as if we were in a Sunday afternoon session, he delivered a lecture on temperance, doing things in moderation, etc. He did not condemn us or condone our actions. Following his monologue, Reverend King gave the container back. He did not indulge. I shall always remember that day.

While a student in college, I had the opportunity to associate with Reverend King personally. I became one of several drivers for him. I drove Reverend King to various churches and special engagements.

There is an element in the Black preaching tradition known as whooping, crooning, or tuning. The terms basically mean the same thing. When preaching to a predominantly Black audience, there is often dialogue between the preacher and the congregation. When the preacher makes a strong point, listeners will say something comparable to: "That's right, Reverend." "Preach it, brother." "Make it plain to us." or "Tell the truth."

After the preacher has been illuminating the text for twenty or thirty minutes, worshippers will began to say something like: "Bring it home, Reverend." "Tune up, Doctor."

These two phrases suggest to the preacher that the worshippers have reached a high spiritual realm and are ready for the minister to conclude the sermon. Urging a conclusion does not mean the people are tired and ready for the preacher to be seated. What they are ready for is a type of worship celebration that is directly linked to the preaching event and is unique to the Black experience.

In this concluding moment of the sermon the minister attempts to pull together all that has been said in a celebratory manner. It is the climax. The concluding moments end with a type of spiritual celebration. The preacher and the worshippers at this stage are usually caught up in the spirit. It is at this stage that people in the congregation usually get happy. The preacher begins to preach in a rhythmic tone. He and his worshippers literally enter another sphere. Practically everyone present gets caught up in the joy of the moment.

Well, I was with Reverend King when he preached at Sixteenth Street Baptist Church, Birmingham, Alabama. The occasion was the Women's Capital State Convention. The sermon was moving as always. It was vintage King. However, I was stunned when near the end of his sermon my pastor began to whoop. I had never seen or heard him preach in that manner. That was highly unlike him. However, as I stated earlier, in the concluding moment something inexplicable happens between the people and the preacher.

After the service, I said: "Reverend King, you whooped today." I paused and added: "I have never heard you whoop at Dexter."

"Well," he began with a smile, "the sisters at Dexter never talk to me when I am preaching like the old sisters did here today."

As time elapsed and Reverend King's ministry continued, the movement started. The civil rights struggle loomed over the South.

My father, the late Richard Jordan, Sr., was a Pullman porter and so was Mr. E. D. Nixon. Both men were members of the Brotherhood of Sleeping Car Porters.

After the struggle of Black people commenced in Montgomery with the bus boycott, mass meetings were held weekly. The local white establishment tried to crush our efforts. It was difficult to stop events, so a variety of means were employed to weaken the zeal of the Black people and the leadership. For example, white merchants and business people cut off credit to Black folk. Our bank records and accounts were inventoried. Prior to this period white people had not paid much attention to the banking activities of the Black population in Montgomery. It was after they began to examine our accounts that it became clear to them that Black people in Montgomery had a considerable amount of money.

A plan was devised to have the money of the movement exported from the city of Montgomery. The leadership did not want the local white people to know how much was at our command. Reverend King and Mr. Nixon asked me and my father to become night-riders. Reverend King and Mr. Nixon set up what was dubbed The Pony Express. My father and I agreed to be night-riders. We were not the only riders. Several churches provided night-riders. The Jordans were not representatives from Dexter

Avenue Baptist Church. My father and I were supporters of the movement and were willing to do whatever we could to advance the cause. Each Pony Express team was briefed ahead of time and knew when its turn came around.

Our duty was one of great responsibility and was not taken lightly. Initially the mass meetings were held on Monday nights. A collection was always taken to help support the boycott and the movement in general. After the monies had been counted, the cash was handed over to the Pony Express. Money was coming in from all over the country to support the movement. The Pony Express would transport thousands of dollars weekly to Columbus, Georgia. In Columbus we had a rendezvous with a designated driver from Georgia. That night-rider would take the monies on to Atlanta, Georgia, where it was deposited in the Citizens Trust Bank. Citizens Trust was only one of several Black banks at that time.

The Pony Express never used the same route two weeks in a row. We traveled alternate roads. Various automobiles were also employed. We never drove the same car twice. We made arrangements with individuals and relatives to use their vehicles at designated times.

Monies continued to come from outside of Montgomery and Alabama to help support the movement. These and all monies were used in specific ways: e.g. to help buy station wagons to transport those who joined the boycott, to buy gas for the vehicles, to assist with repairs of bombed churches, and other similar acts.

My father believed in the movement and what it pointed to regarding the future. He was committed and overtly displayed his conviction.

In fact, my father was so involved in the movement until one day Reverend King called him aside and said: "Brother Jordan, we need all kinds of people to work in the movement. You have four sons. I don't want the movement to harm you or your boys."

Reverend King suggested that my father curb his open activities.

My father was also one of the first to testify in Judge Walter B. Jones' court on how Black people were treated when trying to vote. His testimony was so powerful and graphic that it made an edition of *Time* magazine. I have the magazine at home now among many other collectibles from that era.

Mr. E. D. Nixon separated himself from the movement. He knew and accepted the fact that Reverend King was better qualified intellectually to guide the movement. At the outset Mr. Nixon was a strong King supporter. However, Mr. Nixon began to feel that the Montgomery Improvement Association was not giving him his due credit. He felt that his earlier work, for the rights of Black people, was now being ignored. Indeed Mr. Nixon's pre-King labors were being overshadowed by activities taking place in the King era in Montgomery. However, none of the overshadowing was intentional. An unprecedented historical event was taking place in the nation and all eyes, cameras, and microphones were suddenly shifted in the direction of the leader, who was Reverend King.

There were some individuals who were not professionally obligated to the white power structure. These could participate in the movement without it costing their families. Other Black people, however, could have participated in the movement and it would have been very costly for them. Reverend King had a clear understanding of events and activities. For example, he was always sympathetic toward those who wanted to do more for the movement but their employment, job, or position forced them to have second thoughts. Reverend King never criticized this element. He was practical about the situation.

On the other hand he was not sympathetic toward those Black persons who were fortunate enough to have secured a good education and employment, but wanted to hold back the movement or reduce the pace to a crawl for their own gain. Even some of his church officers and members irritated him along these lines. He expected more from the educated mind or the elite among the race.

The white establishment could not get to Reverend King. Numerous attempts were made. He was threatened, harassed, jailed, offered money, and a host of other activities were implemented to force him to abandon or at least curb his work. Unable to get to Reverend King directly the establishment discovered another path that indirectly led to him. This indirect method served the same purpose. The establishment labored to get to Reverend King through the church.

Some of the members and officials of Dexter Avenue Baptist Church were leading educators in the city. Like Black professionals and educators in other churches, some in Dexter did not want to be harassed or dismissed from places of employment. Individuals began to curb their activities. Family members asked persons in their family to put some distance between themselves and Reverend King.

This was not the whole case. There were many educators from Dexter and numerous other churches who were behind Reverend King and remained supporters. They did not curb their activities or lessen their participation in the movement. Members of this class were willing to take what came, i.e. loss of employment, having to relocate, etc. This element felt it was better to lose personally in order to obtain greater gains for the race and humanity than to gain personally and let humanity and the race's loss be incalculable.

Reverend King decided to leave Montgomery. We had become very close over the years. He had made an indelible impression on me as a college student and young man. His trust in me to be a rider with The Pony Express meant much to me as an individual.

I could always talk to Reverend King. As a parishioner, supporter of the movement, friend, and fraternity brother, I just came right out one day and asked: "Reverend King, why are you leaving Montgomery and Dexter?"

"Well," he began, "I need to broaden my horizons. The movement has outgrown Montgomery. We need to be centrally located in order to be able to flex our muscles."

This was the philosophical answer. I knew better. I was young, but I had been close to him and the movement long enough to know there was more to his decision than he expressed to me.

Some of the leaders of the movement and open supporters began to withdraw from Reverend King. His Montgomery power base was beginning to weaken. People were not distancing themselves from him because they really wanted to withdraw. Pressure from certain corners forced them to put some distance between themselves and Reverend King.

Reverend King probably would have remained in Montgomery. He was fearless. Those who can secure some of his earlier pictures should look at his eyes. They will behold the eyes of a fearless man. However, a fearless man with a weakening power base could not have forged ahead as Reverend King had done up until 1959/60.

There was a power in Reverend King's countenance. He carried himself in a manner with which many, especially his opponents, could not deal. A force greater than Reverend King moved him. When he spoke, there was a voice greater than his voice. He had something within. There were times when I honestly thought he should have slowed down. Events were always taking place fast. That force kept him going and guided Reverend King.

Reverend King left one piece of unfinished business at Dexter Avenue Baptist Church which I know he had a strong desire to see completed. The dream he left on the drawing board was that of a church library. He said on one occasion: "Every church needs a library. It is needed especially for those who come behind so they will know what went on before."

I believe Reverend King wanted Dexter Avenue Baptist Church to develop more spiritually and more persons from our congregation to go out and render greater service for Christ Jesus our Lord. He said in a sermon: "Any church that does not produce out of its membership a pastor at least once every fifty years is a dying church and might need to close its doors."

I am well over fifty years of age and have been in Dexter all of my life. The only pastor I am aware of who has come out of that congregation in the past fifty years is Thomas Jordan, pastor of Lily Baptist Church, Montgomery, Alabama. Thomas is my younger brother.

If I had to succinctly describe Reverend King, I would say: "He was the Moses of our time sent by God."

Mrs. Viola Howze Jordan

Richard and I were undergraduate students at Alabama State College together. He was a member of Dexter Avenue Baptist Church. He invited me to attend a worship service with him one Sunday. After that Sunday, he took me often. I enjoyed worshipping at Dexter. The church was always packed. Reverend King never had a manuscript. He would just stand up and start talking. Those in the audience remained spellbound until the discourse was completed.

After completing all my academic requirements, I received my bachelor's degree. Richard and I were married in 1957. We were a young struggling couple facing all of the challenges newlyweds encounter. We were trying to get on our feet.

Our first home was located at 919 East Grove Street. One day there was a knock at the door. We had no idea who it was or what the visit concerned. To our surprise it was Reverend and Mrs. King standing on the front porch. Richard and I invited them in. Their visit alone was very meaningful. However, once in the house Reverend and Mrs. King said they had stopped by to say hello and give us a wedding gift. The Kings gave us a silver butter dish. They sat for a little while and talked with us, then departed.

We still have that silver butter dish. It has become a family treasure.

When I became Mrs. Jordan, I decided to unite with my husband's church. One Sunday, following the sermon, Reverend King opened the doors of the church. An invitation was extended to any person present who wanted to join Dexter. I went forward. Deacon Robert Nesbitt, Sr., greeted me. He recorded my name and other pertinent information to pass on to the congregation at the proper time. I was baptized earlier in life and was a member of Union Baptist Church, Coffeeville, Alabama. I told Deacon Nesbitt that I was uniting with Dexter on my Christian experience. Reverend King stood by me and expressed his delight with my decision. The pastor told me that I would be given the right hand of fellowship at a later date.

I joined the Young Matrons group. I did not have a driver's license at that time. Richard was involved in the movement as well as church activities. He could not always drive me to my destination. Mrs. King used to come by and pick me up to attend the Matrons' meeting. She was very kind and thoughtful.

Reverend King would stop by occasionally to greet the group and sit for a little while. I remember we had a meeting in the home of Mrs. Gussie Carter. Reverend King stopped by and shared in the repast.

Reverend and Mrs. King loved the community and attended many non-church-related activities. Reverend King especially enjoyed sporting events. I remember Richard and I were at a basketball game at Tuskegee Institute, which was not more than an hour's drive from Montgomery. The game was played in Logan Hall. Reverend and Mrs. King were there also. They came by themselves.

After the game all of us stopped at a small establishment and ate hamburgers, fries, and drank sodas, while laughing and talking the night away. It was an enjoyable basketball game and good Christian fellowship after the event. Reverend and Mrs. King were just good loving down-to-earth people.

Reverend King was an understanding pastor. I say this because of an incident that occurred one Sunday afternoon at church. I was directly involved, as well as one other little person in the Jordan family.

The Jordan family's day was full that Sunday. Following the morning worship service Richard and I attended a dedication ceremony at McIntyre Elementary School. We later had dinner, after which it was time to return to church for evening worship. Our first born, Sharon, was about eighteen months old at the time. She had been with us all day and did not get a full nap. By evening she had become very irritable. It had indeed been a long day. Richard and I were somewhat tired ourselves.

Following the hymns, scripture, and prayers, Reverend King started to deliver his evening sermon. As he was preaching, Sharon began to give signs of being tired and sleepy. She was rather loud. Dexter was not a large facility and sound carried well in the sanctuary. I was doing my best as a young mother to comfort Sharon. I was achieving minimal results. Perhaps the pastor saw the concern on my face. Looking down from the pulpit at me, Reverend King said out loud: "Leave her alone. She is just a baby."

His words calmed me. Reverend King resumed his sermon and the worship service continued. I was able to relax and listen to the sermon.

Reverend and Mrs. King left Montgomery. Their love and concern spanned the distance between Atlanta and Montgomery. Richard and I received a Christmas communication from them annually for many years after their departure.

Reverend King returned to Alabama in 1965 to lead the Selma to Montgomery March. The marchers were to arrive in Montgomery the end of the week, Friday. I was pregnant with my second child. I went into labor that morning. Richard took me to the hospital. I remained at the hospital for a long time. My doctor said: "The baby is not coming today. Today is my anniversary. You can go home and wait."

We returned home. I tried to rest, but could not. The labor pains did not lessen. They increased as the day went by. In the late evening I told Richard: "You need to take me back to the hospital."

We got in the car and he took me back to Saint Jude Hospital. The marchers had already completed the march. The big rally downtown in front of the capitol had ended. A big affair was being held on the grounds of Saint Jude School. Many famous personalities, Black and white, were on the program. I gave natural birth to our second daughter late that evening.

Because I gave birth on the grounds where the Selma to Montgomery closing rally was being held Richard said enthusiastically:

"Let's name her Freedom."

I was less enthused with the suggested name. Richard had worked closely with Reverend King when the latter was in Montgomery. As a family, we had lived through some trying and challenging years up until 1965. Black people had accomplished much during that time. I readily understood my husband's yearning to give our second daughter a name that would bring to mind memories of the struggle. The name had to be linked with and have the sound of freedom. The child was named LaFreeda Jordan.

Deacon Richmond Smiley

Before providing my reflections on Dr. King I will return to the era of Pastor Vernon Johns. Prior to the resignation of Pastor Johns some friction had developed between him and the Dexter congregation. It was not nearly as strained or ugly as television presents. The friction, in my opinion, developed because of his thinking. It was so advanced compared to our thinking. It was difficult to grasp what he was saying or trying to get us to envision. Pastor Johns' patience was very short. Johns knew where he was going and the undeniable truth of his assertions regarding the social environment of the early 1950s. If you did not get on board, his patience would fly and he would lose his temper. My brother was on the trustee board. I was not a deacon at that time, but I was well aware of events based on information from an eyewitness. Pastor Johns' choice of words after losing his temper was not always the best.

Looking back, I am convinced that Johns' presence among us was providential. God was moving and preparing the way for events which we could not foresee at the time. God had to arouse us for the coming events. Dr. Johns did just that. He was the preacher who began to shake us in our sleep and say: "Wake up. A new day is dawning."

I was born and reared in Montgomery, and to hear someone say, "You do not have to accept segregation," was foreign. Like thousands of others, I used to put my coins in the receptacle and move to the back of the bus. It was a way of life and we never thought otherwise. Those living through that experience simply did not realize how bad and dehumanizing it was. I did not like the practices that accompanied segregation, but I observed them. Reverend Johns told us that we did not have to accept it. Pastor Johns did not accept it and that was why he had no difficulty telling us that we did not have to honor segregation.

Dr. Johns was a practical man. For example, he told us to plant our own gardens, rather than purchase vegetables. By planting one's own garden, a person would save monies that would otherwise be spent. Moreover, when planting one's own garden, he or she could in turn plant extras to sell as a way of earning money. One Sunday Pastor Johns brought to the pulpit collard greens, cabbage, and other eatables from his garden. The dirt, God's rich beautiful soil, was still on them. Why did the pastor bring dirt into the pulpit? He was trying to show us we could be independent and not have to rely on, or purchase from, white people. By growing ourselves we would become independent and sell to each other and to the whites. Pastor Johns started Farming City Enterprise in order to help his people break free of whites. One member of our church, Deacon

Moore, owned a truck farm and sold on a large scale. Deacon Moore was doing what Johns envisioned us implementing on a larger scale. There is no doubt that Pastor Johns roused us from our social slumbering.

Dexter Avenue Baptist Church had a history of not keeping a minister for an extended period. Pastor Johns, the great one, left. "Who are we going to get?" the congregation wondered. We were running ahead of the Lord. Dexter was without a pastor for a considerable length of time, but all went well during the interim. We interviewed candidates for a long time. The transition from Johns to King was not as swift as television portrays. A great deal of what I have seen in media productions, regarding Johns, King, and Dexter Avenue Baptist Church, is inaccurate.

Pastor Johns' pastorate was not very harmonious, but it was not violent either. The church was slowly getting in tempo with Johns' principles and teachings. We were gradually coming to embrace his philosophy. Then, as it happened, he resigned. However, Pastor Johns had resigned his position as pastor on numerous occasions. He would get angry, walk out of the pulpit, then return and preach one of the best theologically sound sermons ever heard.

Dr. King came to preach at a church known for not keeping a minister very long. One or two deacons were very outspoken and wanted to run things. Daddy King, Martin Luther King, Jr.'s father, knew the deacons by name and told the son: "You don't want to take that church." However, the young King accepted our call to be pastor.

We were accustomed to Pastor Johns quoting scripture and paraphrasing so listeners could understand and grasp the message. Dr. Johns was the greatest speaker we knew. "Who can rival Johns?" we mused. However, the minute we heard Reverend King we knew "this was the man!" After hearing King, the church's only concern was—"Could we afford him?"

I have never met a person as genuine as Martin Luther King, Jr. He never thought of himself. He did what the Lord told him to do and was not afraid.

So many things impressed me about Pastor King. The first time I was impressed with him was when I heard him preach. I was immediately convinced that there was something special about him.

On another occasion I was deeply moved by his actions. It was at the Annual Church Conference, during one of Pastor King's early years. The conference was always held in December. At this conference the pastor laid out his program for the coming year. This particular year Mrs. King was at the hospital. A Dexter deacon, Dr. W. D. Pettus, was Mrs. King's physician. During the midst of the conference, Dr. Pettus called the church to inform Pastor King that Mrs. King had given birth. Initially we had no idea that Mrs. King was in labor. We urged Reverend King to adjourn the meeting and go to the hospital, but he stayed and laid out his plan for the church for the coming year.

Early during Dr. King's pastorate of Dexter, Mrs. Parks was arrested. Mr. E. D. Nixon got her out of jail and was instrumental in calling a meeting. Mr. Nixon called selected preachers and citizens together. They met at Dexter. So much has happened in the basement of this church. Mr. Nixon, based on logical consideration, should have headed the organization. He was one of the premier political leaders in the community. I cannot say why he did not assume the leadership role. I do not think it was in the Lord's plan. Many meetings had been called, many people killed, and all previous meetings, regardless of how promising, fizzled out. Nothing extraordinary happened. We thought the plans developed in this meeting would fizzle out also.

In retrospect, I can say Mr. Nixon could not have led such a movement. That is no reflection of the man in any way and is not said in a derogatory vain. Pastor Johns could not have led such a movement. He was too hot-tempered.

Dr. King was mild-mannered, but thorough. I cannot say how it came down to King being the leader. The experience of other ministers in the city of Montgomery who pastored large congregations, their seniority, and longevity should have confirmed one of them as the leader. However, they selected our pastor.

This was when the closeness between Reverend King and myself began to develop.

In the beginning I had doubts about the movement. "Could we pull this off? Would the 40,000 Black people whose means of transportation to their jobs, and almost everywhere else, was the bus sustain the hardships that would necessarily develop with not riding the bus?" I wondered. The boycott of the Montgomery bus service started in December. The days were short and the weather terrible. That was why I wondered whether we could successfully accomplish the mission. Many others entertained the same notion. To our amazement it all started coming together. Taxi drivers started picking up people and carrying them to their destination. The organization provided transportation.

My office was one block from Holt Street Baptist Church. I dropped my son off at the church nursery each morning. Then I drove my six riders to their destinations. All six of my riders were domestic workers in the Cloverdale section of Montgomery.

I remember one lady who I transported saying one morning to the others that she had been threatened by her white employer. The threat was to terminate her service.

"She asked the other day did I ride the bus to work. I said no. Someone picked me up," the rider told her co-riders.

The others in the car also told similar stories of out-witting employers. Shortly thereafter the lady first mentioned was fired by her employer. However, before being fired someone else hired her.

I was self-employed and near a telephone all the time. I was easy to reach. I could always get away for a few minutes. This was how I became one of Pastor King's primary drivers. If the pastor needed to get to the airport immediately, he would telephone me. Brother Roscoe Williams was also self-employed. He was an electrician. Pastor King telephoned him sometime. I was more accessible than Brother Williams. Sometimes the latter would be out on a job and could not get away.

It was from driving Dr. King around that I realized things were getting bad. The pastor had no time to himself. His telephone rang all of the time. Sometimes it was people needing help on the telephone. Other times threats were being voiced. I saw what my pastor was confronting. I extended an invitation to him to come out to my house and relax. He needed rest and time to himself. He accepted the offer from me and my wife. His first period of relaxation at our home was beneficial and Dr. King repeated this act on many occasions.

Pastor King often told me my faith was limited. Why? Well, for example, I would not let him go out without my exiting the house first to look around. I did not want anything to happen to him while in my company. He teased me about it often, but deep down inside I do not think he minded. I usually knew his whereabouts. Whenever his schedule changed, the secretary alerted me.

There is so much I understand now, but did not back then. The night his home was bombed was an occasion when anyone would have been angry. He was at a mass meeting that evening. Brother Williams and I were driving him that night. We rushed him home to the parsonage on Jackson Street. Upon arriving, Dr. King hurried inside. Mrs. King, the baby, and Mrs. Williams, Brother Williams' wife, were safe. A crowd of supporters was slowly gathering in the front of the Kings' home. They were angry. We could hear the noise inside. I slipped out the back door of the house and made my way in the dark to the front. I saw hundreds and hundreds of Black people standing with shotguns, knives, and weapons. They did not hide their weapons. They were ready to act on behalf of Dr. King and his family. "What is going to happen?" I mused. The people were crying, cursing, and expressing their dismay. I did not want Pastor King to come outside and was going back inside to convince him to remain in the house. Black and white people wanted him destroyed. I thought perhaps one had been planted in the crowd and might kill him.

As I prepared to turn around and retrace my steps in the dark to the back door of the parsonage, I could not believe my eyes. I saw Pastor King standing on the porch. It was too late to try to stop him.

I could not do anything. I stood and watched, not having the slightest idea what was going to happen. He raised his hands and said: "May I have your attention please." I thought to myself—"These people are angry." To my amazement a hush came over the crowd. "I know you are concerned for me," pastor began. "My wife is fine. My child is fine. Go home and put your weapons away. Join me tomorrow morning and we will continue this protest peacefully."

In a matter of minutes the crowd dispersed. Pastor King had that much influence. By this time people knew he was totally dedicated to completing a mission for them and not for himself.

I admired Dr. King's ability to lead people, but in so doing the people being led thought they were in control. He would bring out the best in people, and put himself in the background. "Good idea," he would often say.

When there were important decisions to be made, people would urge: "Dr. King, you decide. Whatever the decision we are with you."

He would reply: "Oh, no! You must decide."

He was always giving someone else the credit. He would make you think it was your idea and your idea alone.

I was a guinea pig of sorts with Pastor King. He would always mention something to me while riding. I always answered negatively, saying something such as: "Dr. King, please don't do that."

In practically every instance he did the opposite. My concern was always his safety and not the idea itself. For example, he opposed the Vietnam War. He did not run that by me. I heard about that on the news. I could not understand why he would take on that issue, the war, with all of the other concerns that demanded his attention. I saw him opposing the war as one more matter to take up his time and energy. The secretary telephoned one day and told me what time the pastor was to arrive at the Montgomery Airport.

I had decided to read Pastor King the riot act regarding his statement on the war. I just felt he did not need to take that on. While driving from the airport, I began reading him the riot act. However, Pastor King straightened me out quickly.

"I believe the war is wrong," he revealed, "and if I am going to be the moral conscience of the nation I have to say it. I have to do the right thing."

Looking back I should have known better than to do what I did riding from the airport.

The president of Fisk University, Dr. Johnson, came to talk to Pastor King about accepting the presidency of Fisk. Dr. Johnson was preparing to retire. Dr. King asked me shortly after his conference with Dr. Johnson: "Brother Richmond, what do you think your pastor should do?"

In the warm title to which I often referred to him when we talked, I said: "Brother Pastor, as much as I would hate to see you leave Dexter, you cannot turn this down."

Pastor King made me feel a little bad when he responded: "Brother Richmond, you have to get your focus in life together. That is not my calling. My calling is to be a pastor. Being the president of a great college would be good, but I could not say what needed to be said. My hands would be tied. People give endowments to schools and I would have to guard my words. I cannot live like that."

I think he would have liked the presidency of Fisk, but Pastor King was too committed. His whole outlook was to the mission that had been entrusted to him.

When he went on speaking engagements, people gave him large honorariums. They really wanted him to keep the money, but he gave it to the movement. People came to trust him. People thoroughly trusted him.

Dr. King's caring for people was beyond all that one can imagine. There could be an important meeting with distinguished people that could have affected the outcome of the struggle and I would be trying my best to get Pastor King to the destination. However, he always stopped if someone, whether he knew them or not, said: "Dr. King, I need to talk to you."

I would be so angry thinking: "This person is not talking about anything worthwhile. We need to get on to the meeting." But not King. If a person had a problem, King had an ear. Strangers walking up to him straight off of the street received the same pastoral attention. Everybody could talk to him. He could not always help, but he would always listen. I never knew anyone to talk to him and walk away in sorrow. He never minimized the difficulty of the hour. "I am here with you," he assured the people. They believed it. After the commencement of the movement, we were convinced he could pull it off. Initially people did not want to do it, but after seeing him and his commitment they were determined to see it through.

Whenever he was in a crowd, I became concerned for Reverend King's safety. My interest in his welfare increased after he was stabbed in New York. I remember the Sunday it was announced that he had been stabbed. Dexter Avenue Baptist Church was packed and there was not a dry eye among us.

Always at the darkest hour during the movement, God would do something to assure us of the presence of the Eternal. The police chief or mayor would say something ridiculous and unify the people. Once I picked Pastor King up from jail when he was arrested in Montgomery. He said: "A white policeman aided me while I was in jail. The man told me 'I want you to know that nobody is going to hit you or harm you. I can't get you out or be a spokesman for you; but I will stay here with you.' Brother Richmond, you do not know what a good feeling that was."

I never met a man so committed to others. He gave of his time, his resources and of self, totally to others. He never thought about what he could have done for himself. This was the man as I knew him. A man and pastor who was a joy to be around.

Horrible and threatening episodes were constantly taking place around us that were frightening. It was easy to become depressed, but not around Pastor King. During seriously tense moments, when he sensed people were getting depressed, Pastor King consistently came up with some lighthearted statement to ease their anxiety. Instead of people keeping his spirits up, he kept our spirits up.

Reverend King loved Dexter Avenue Baptist Church. Whenever he returned from a trip, the first words out of his mouth as we departed the airport were: "Is all well at Dexter? Does anyone need me?"

I would report or whoever picked him up would pass on details. He would say: "I must get by there."

We often detoured, after leaving the airport, so he could visit a member.

Much has been written and talked about regarding my pastor's womanizing. I want to go on record telling what I know and observed. I was with pastor on countless occasions. I knew his schedule well. He hardly made a move and I was not somehow involved. I cannot say what did or did not happen. I can say, however, that I was with Pastor King in some close places where women did everything they could to tempt him and he handled himself as a perfect gentleman. He did not make the woman feel bad.

I recall one night a woman was determined to get him out of my car to ride with her. She was one of the most beautiful women I have ever seen. He said: "No, no, you don't mean that. I know you are joking. You don't want me to ride with you."

He did not embarrass her in any way. If I had possession of a tape recorder that night, I could have taped that conversation, edited it, and made that dialogue sound like anything I wanted it to be and sound like.

He was human. Some women perhaps did learn of his presence in a town and secured a room in the same hotel. I don't know what happened on those occasions. One thing I do know—Pastor King remained focused and led us through to the end.

Pastor King and I were together often. I took great delight in driving him around. He shared a lot with me that I will never tell anyone. Those things were told to me in secret, pastor to parishioner, brother to brother. He embraced me as a confidant. That is what I do not understand about his close friends and allies. I am sure he confided in many of them. Nevertheless they have written books and revealed confidential information. They did it, I guess, for money. I have a problem with those who exploit events for personal gain.

Dr. King decided to resign the pastorate at Dexter Avenue Baptist Church. I think there were two reasons for his departure. First, he saw his work, ministry, and mission to humanity expanding. Flights in and out of Montgomery were infrequent back then. Dr. King could not go and come as he wished. The second reason for his departure, in my opinion, was because of his genuine pastoral concern for the Dexter flock. The membership suggested that he just go as his schedule demanded and arrange for another minister to preach. However, Pastor King did not want to short-change the congregation. He loved Dexter Avenue Baptist Church. Pastor King came to us as a full-time pastor and felt anything less was unfair to the Dexter flock.

Dr. King returned to Montgomery several times after having resigned the pastorate at Dexter.

One of those occasions was after receiving the Nobel Peace Prize in 1964. Thousands of dollars were involved. I do not know exactly how much Dr. King received. I had the feeling, however, that he was going to give his share of the money away. I was to pick him up from the airport. I had developed a strategy regarding the money. I was going to reveal the strategy to Pastor King when I picked him up. My strategy was, as I said to him later: "Brother Pastor, keep some of that money for your family. I know you are going to give some of it away."

Pastor cut me down. He explained that the prize was not Martin Luther King, Jr.'s, but belonged to the movement. The prize was not his. It belonged to the people. He gave the money to the movement.

Another occasion which brought him back to Montgomery was the Selma to Montgomery March in 1965. After the Selma march, Pastor King stayed at my house. A white lady, Mrs. Liuzzo, who provided transportation and aided the movement, was killed. Pastor King was scheduled to fly out of Montgomery. I went to the airport and made arrangements for him to enter the facility from the side. I returned home and picked him up. As we rode up to the airport, someone recognized him and shouted: "Dr. King, Dr. King...."

That was it. Everyone wanted to talk. He began to converse with the people.

"You have to catch a plane," I reminded.

Dr. King was unmoved by my reminder. He kept talking with the people and did not miss his flight.

Dr. King was invited by Alabama State College to return to Montgomery and speak. I picked him up at the airport for that engagement.

"Pastor King, do you want to stay in the hotel or at our house?" I inquired.

The room was already paid for by his host. Dr. King smiled and said: "Brother Richmond, I would love to stay at your house."

We never went to the hotel.

It was no surprise to me that when called to Memphis to help the garbage collectors he went to their aid.

Mrs. Jean Smiley

Reverend King was one of the nicest individuals I have ever met. As a young pastor, he labored to get young adults involved in Dexter Avenue Baptist Church. He organized the Young Matrons and the Month Clubs (Birth Month Clubs). The Young Matrons were in their early 20s and 30s. Coretta was part of the group and served as a leader of sorts. We discussed and committed ourselves to doing things in the church. Dr. King called on the Young Matrons to render a variety of services.

His sermons were always very dramatic. He had excellent points to share with the congregation. His sermons were food for thought and people were there to enjoy the feast and soak it up each Sunday.

After the movement began, he tried to express how the people should conduct themselves in light of the scriptures.

I was surprised one day when the pastor telephoned my home. That familiar voice that I heard each Sunday rang out. Dr. King asked me to be the superintendent of the annual Vacation Bible School. I explained to him that I could not possibly undertake such an awesome responsibility. I did not feel adequate.

"Oh, yes, you can. Yes, you can," I recall him saying.

No amount of explaining on my part, however, was sufficient. The pastor refused to take no for an answer. He obviously felt I could handle it. His philosophy was that a person could do anything he or she made up in his or her mind to do. By the time our conversation ended a few minutes later I had committed myself to being the superintendent for Dexter's annual Vacation Bible School. Afterward he would always tease me about thinking I could not, but I did so well.

There is a photograph in the church library from that year. In the photograph seated and standing on the front steps of Dexter Avenue Baptist Church are the Vacation Bible School staff, students, and Reverend King. Whenever I see that photograph many memories come to mind.

Dr. King always made time to greet and speak to everyone within his immediate view.

My grandfather and Dr. King were born on January 15th. One year we had a party for the two of them at the home of my uncle. The pastor was informed and arrived at the appropriate time. Dr. King had only been there a short while before the telephone rang. It was for the pastor. To his and our disappointment he had to leave. Before leaving Dr. King thanked us and explained that duty called. He departed before we could sing happy birthday. We did sing to my grandfather.

After leaving Dexter and the city, Reverend King returned several years later to lead the Selma to Montgomery March. I was teaching school in Montgomery County. School officials would not release us so I left work early. I came to the church. It was well guarded. My father, Deacon Robert Nesbitt, Sr., was inside. I managed to get inside. Dr. and Mrs. King came in shortly thereafter. They were tired. That much was apparent. Nevertheless Reverend King, like always, took time to greet everyone in the lower level of the church as he entered. He greeted me, gave me a kiss on the cheek, smiled, and said: "Here is my little superintendent."

We all loved Dr. King. All of the groups to which I belonged would pray for him. I was very disturbed when I heard he had been assassinated.

Dr. John Porter

I am at present the pastor of Sixth Avenue Baptist Church, Birmingham, Alabama. My ministry with this congregation has spanned more than thirty years.

I met Reverend King on the campus of Alabama State College. I was introduced to Reverend King by Dr. Roosevelt Crockett, who was the professor of philosophy at the college. Dr. Crockett introduced me as a young minister. This was my senior year of college which was 1954.

No activities had commenced in Montgomery and Reverend King was just a local pastor doing the Lord's will at Dexter Avenue Baptist Church. Reverend King informed me that he did not have a helper.

"Would you like to come and work with me?" he asked on the spot.

Reverend King desired assistance. There were not many candidates who felt comfortable going to Dexter. They would have gotten unnerved.

I was working with another pastor at the time. However, I seized the opportunity to work with this young highly educated minister. Black preachers of his academic caliber, especially in Alabama, were indeed rare at that time. I determined that this was a rare opportunity.

I welcomed the opportunity to work with Reverend King for two reasons. First he was a young seminary-trained man. Secondly he was a new image of a preacher. It was important for me to have this new image. I was thoroughly acquainted with the old Black preacher, who was great and played a valuable role in the Black community. However, in Reverend King I saw all of the dedication, richness, and power of the old Black preacher plus much more. For example, Reverend King did not talk like a preacher. He used an easy conversational voice and never spoke at certain times in a preacher's tone.

His dress was impeccable. He was always well dressed, but in a simple way. It was like an English style, nothing flashy. Reverend King's whole spirit was one of humbleness. Preachers have enormous egos. Reverend King did not.

Reverend King's father, known to the preaching community as Daddy King, preached the installation sermon of his son at Dexter Avenue Baptist Church. He affectionately called his son M. L. I remember Daddy King saying in the installation sermon: "M. L. if you can help it, don't preach." In a more emphatic voice he reiterated: "M. L. if you can help it, don't preach." The senior King moved closer to his son and said: "M L. if you can help it, don't preach." Then in a low voice, but loud enough for others to hear he added: "But I hope you can't help it."

I remember that clearly to this day.

My work with Reverend King was enjoyable. I was impressed with Reverend King's organizational skills. He was well organized as a pastor. He was the epitome of a church organizer.

I was awed by his preaching. He wrote his sermons out, but preached without a manuscript or notes. His manuscript was always left behind. Impressed by this method I tried it. I only did it once. It did not work for me. There was a pathos in his voice. He was always serious. There was never anything frivolous in his discourses. He had a very inquisitive mind.

After Sunday evening worship service, Reverend King would take me back to the campus. First he would put Mrs. King out at the parsonage and see her in. Then he would take me to the campus. He used Sunday evenings after service as a time to visit his members. Reverend King would go from one home to another. He was still going back and forth to Boston University. I often felt he should have been at home with Mrs. King since he sometimes had to return to Boston early during the week. It was at this time that I first became aware of the importance of the pastor going to the home of parishioners.

Dexter was an affluent church. However, the one lesson I learned under Reverend King's leadership was that members of affluent churches also appreciated pastoral visits.

After preaching a high-powered sermon, a preacher has to wind down. Reverend King also used his Sunday evening home visits as a winding-down period. On many Sunday evenings he taught a Bible study class.

Reverend King had a clarity about the pastorate. Occasionally he was absent on Sunday. Some members felt that he should pay his substitute, as was the custom in those days at some churches. I remember Reverend King saying to all interested parties: "You are alluding to my position as a 11:00 a.m.-12:00 job on Sunday. I hold the position of pastor all week."

Reverend King was a hard-working, diligent pastor who took his duties seriously. He visited members, visited the sick, and did all of the traditional pastoral duties. His rebuttal was terse and clear. All listeners understood what he was saying. Reverend King was clear in his mind about who a pastor was, the role of a pastor, and what being a pastor was about.

The only concern I recall Reverend King expressing to me was regarding the choir. There were several music majors in the choir. Some choir members felt they did not need to come to rehearsal. However, the type of music the choir wanted to sing required practice.

He was only two or three years older than I, but I never called him Martin. He was a formal person. Reverend King was not an aloof or standoffish type person. He was warm and friendly, but reserved.

Reverend King bestowed a great honor on me as a young clergyman. Once he had to catch a plane and go out of town. He conducted a funeral, but was unable to accompany the family to the cemetery. He asked me to go to the cemetery in his stead and commit the remains. I was awestruck. Pastors hold some official duties close and execute those acts themselves. I was more honored than surprised at his offer. This was the first time to commit the remains of a deceased for me.

Since it was my first occasion, this event was a learning experience. At the cemetery when the family began to wail and weep and the offspring called their deceased mother I got a lump in my throat. I realized on this occasion that under such circumstances the minister had to try and maintain his composure.

Reverend King allowed me to share in Sunday morning pulpit events. I would read the morning scripture or pray. He gave me opportunities to preach also. Reverend King allowed me to preach once a month. While completing his dissertation, Reverend King made every effort to be in Montgomery on weekends.

Reverend King expected my relationship with Dexter Avenue Baptist Church to be professional. He served the college community also. Sometimes there were demonstrations on campus such as students protesting against the dining hall. I was often in the middle of events. Reverend King spoke to me about my activities. He explained that Dexter's relationship with Alabama State College was very close. Dexter and the College were intertwined. I was reminded by Reverend King that I should not get too far out of line with my student activities because as his assistant I represented Dexter Avenue Baptist Church.

Reverend King was very generous to young ministers. He gave me the opportunity to work with him during his first year at Dexter. I graduated and a friend of mine, Harold Carter, was given the same opportunity the next school year. Three years later another young preacher on the campus of Alabama State College was extended the same kindness. His name was T. Y. Rogers.

The bus boycott and the movement started. As the leader, Reverend King had a monumental task. He was called to lead some fiery individuals who were very difficult to guide. However, he could undress them in a meeting with his humility.

People elevated him. He was their leader. However, Reverend King was always amazed and awed by this elevation. He never thought of himself or saw himself as anyone more than a humble servant.

I vividly recollect being at a mass meeting with him one night. After the event concluded, an old lady rushed up to Reverend King, threw herself to the floor of the church, reposed at his feet, and wrapped her arms around his legs. The old lady had probably been a victim of oppression in Montgomery for decades and considered Reverend King a religious champion for her cause as well as the cause of tens of thousands of other Black people in Montgomery. Reverend King was moved by the woman's honest display of her affections regarding his place in her heart and the hearts of countless others. He stood speechless—stunned beyond words. Reverend King was embarrassed by the woman's actions. After a moment, he collected himself. Reverend King reached down and lifted the old gray haired woman to her feet. She rose slowly. When standing, he hugged her. No words needed to be spoken by either party.

Dr. King's greatest strength, in my opinion, was his humility.

Mrs. Bertha P. Williams

I grew up in Dexter Avenue Baptist Church.

My husband and I were at Dexter during the ministry of Dr. Vernon Johns. We were very fond of Dr. Johns. He was very flexible. He could talk to the young and the old. I said to myself after Vernon left: "We are going to elect another pastor. Perhaps we should go for a younger man."

When Reverend King was a candidate for the pastorate of the church, we had many young members at the time. That was one reason we wanted him and finally voted for his leadership. Several other ministers came to preach during the time we were without a pastor, but Reverend King became a front runner and no other contenders came close.

Others were also of the opinion that we needed some young blood in the pulpit at Dexter. Most churches do not pay much attention to young folks. Young preachers usually try to meet the spiritual needs of young people.

Even before Reverend King was officially installed as the pastor of Dexter, Mr. E. D. Nixon permitted him to speak at one of the NAACP meetings in Montgomery. Mr. Nixon and Dr. James Pierce were working together. After Reverend King spoke at the NAACP meeting, Mr. Nixon said to some Dexter members: "We need this man in this town. You all might need him at Dexter, but we need him in Montgomery."

Mr. Nixon determined early on that Reverend King could be an asset to the Black community of Montgomery.

The call to be the pastor of Dexter Avenue Baptist Church was formally extended to Reverend King. I remember two pastoral initiatives he undertook shortly after becoming pastor. First he started the Scholarship Program.

Reverend King proposed giving scholarships to worthy high school seniors. He said: "The monies need to be for academic excellence. We are not going to give the monies just for the sake of giving. The monies will not just be given away."

"There are many unmotivated students who would be inspired to produce by the chance of winning the church scholarship," he stated on another occasion.

Reverend King, who had a love for learning himself, proposed that the church scholarship be $500.00. That does not sound like much today, but back in the 1950s $500.00 was a handsome contribution toward a freshman student's tuition.

Some criteria were established. Applicants had to be a member of Dexter Avenue Baptist Church. They had to participate in the church program at Dexter such as Sunday School and Baptist Training Union (BTU). Students had to have an acceptable grade point average. Dexter had good students.

No favoritism was to find its way into the selection process. Though his daughter was a child, at a later time I remember Reverend King saying regarding the selection process: "If it's my daughter, she must participate and meet the requirements."

Secondly Reverend King introduced the idea of a church library.

"You all don't have a library?" he asked on one occasion.

"We have Sunday School literature and such," it was explained to him, "but not an established library."

Reverend King knew that I was a librarian. I was the first Black librarian employed by the city of Montgomery. The pastor asked me and Dr. Zelia Evans to head the library project. The church had no monies immediately available for a library and we could not start as soon as Reverend King desired. Ten months or so after his arrival in Montgomery, Reverend King became busy with the movement and Dr. Evans and myself could not get the library off of the ground. It was his idea and we needed his support.

The bus boycott took off. Reverend King had been with us for less than one year. Reverend King became the elected leader. White opponents tried to crush the movement. They reasoned one of the quickest ways to bring the bus boycott to an end was to strike fear in the leader.

Opponents were calling the home of Reverend King frequently. Often Mrs. King answered the telephone. All sorts of evil, terrifying, and ugly expressions were said to her. Because she was the wife of the leader of the bus boycott Mrs. King necessarily encountered abuses. The ladies from Dexter Avenue Baptist Church who were not afraid arranged to assist Mrs. King. We would go to the parsonage to keep her company and answer the telephone. A schedule was devised and each woman knew her hours. I never saw the list. I only knew my time.

My shift at the library began at twelve o'clock noon during the week. I answered the telephone at the parsonage on certain days from 8:00 a.m. - 11:00 a.m. I heard some horrible language.

One morning a voice filled with hate said: "You tell that Black big nose nigger if he doesn't stop, we will burn his house down and run him out of town."

On another occasion Reverend King was to be told: "If you don't stop these niggers, we are going to blow up your house and the church."

These are just two of numerous such calls I can recount. The two above should suffice because most of the calls had this flavor.

One morning Reverend and Mrs. King were at the breakfast table eating. Yolanda, their first child, had not yet been born. The telephone rang.

"I will get it," I announced.

"I would like to speak to Reverend King," a warm innocent female voice said politely.

I went to the kitchen and told Reverend King he had a telephone call. He excused himself. A few moments later he returned to the kitchen and said: "My, my, I have never heard such terrible language in all of my born days."

I was shocked, but could tell Reverend King was serious about what he had just said.

"I can't imagine a lady talking in such a manner as to upset you so much," I rejoined.

"Well," he began, immediately seeing to the bottom of things. "I talked to a man."

I will never forget what Reverend King said after revealing he had spoken to a man. He said: "When I was first asked to work with the movement, I was afraid because like anybody else I want to live a long time. But before it is over someone will lose his life. It could be me." And then with the assurance of a preacher who knew he had been called of God to fulfill a divine destiny, Reverend King testified: "But I'm going on." I became worried. I did not envision the situation being so serious. A little later Reverend King remarked: "Longevity has its place, if you are doing something."

I left the parsonage at 11:00 a.m. to go to work. I was a bit shaken myself. At work I thought to myself—Reverend King could come out of his house and be gunned down. I never thought people could be so low-down. Reverend King led the movement and labored under the threat of death daily. He never gave signs of being overly concerned. He must have had peace of mind about it all.

After this episode, I noticed a change in the preaching of our pastor. His sermons began to take on a different flavor. The telephone threats were intended to weaken or shake him up. Instead these activities spurred him forward and gave Reverend King greater determination. He began to say in his sermons statements such as: "I am not afraid anymore. This movement must go on."

I specifically remember the above statement being uttered from the pulpit.

Reverend King was young at the time and had to stand under a great deal. He had to have been strong and his faith unshakable to maintain his belief. The average man or preacher would have surrendered.

I went to sit with Mrs. King on certain days. When not with her in the morning, I drove boycotters to and from various locations between 8:00 a.m. - 11:00 a.m. I was not in the organized car pool. I picked up Black people and drove them around when I could.

One day a policeman gave me a ticket. I was in the vicinity of Normandale Shopping Center. It was raining. Some people will probably need a ride, I thought. Otherwise they would probably have had to walk and get wet. I saw two Black ladies come out of a store with some packages. I stopped, blew the horn, and asked: "Do you all need a ride?"

They came to the car and asked:. "Are you in the pool?"

"No," I said, "but I will give you a ride."

The ladies told me they lived in the area of Cleveland Avenue. They were appreciative for the ride. The ladies expounded for two or three minutes about how each thought the pair was going to have to walk home in the rain. I drove out of the shopping center lot. At the first stop light I saw two policemen behind me in my rear view mirror. I said to myself—"I bet they are following me."

When near where the ladies resided, I said: "I can't take you directly to your front doors. I do not want to be charged with picking up passengers without a license."

I put them out at the corner of Jefferson Davis and Cleveland Avenue. About two blocks away from where I put the ladies out I heard a siren and saw flashing lights. I pulled over and waited for the officers to approach.

"Do you know what you did?" one asked, standing by the driver's side of my car.

"No, what did I do?" I had been watching them in my rear view mirror all the time.

"You ran the red light right back there."

"Oh, sir, I did not do that," I said politely. "If I did, you ran it also."

"You don't have to talk to us about it," one said sharply. "We'll give you a ticket and you can take it to Fred Gray."

Mr. Gray was a Black lawyer in town and was Reverend King's attorney.

One night a mass meeting was held at First Baptist Church on Ripley Street. This was the church Reverend Ralph Abernathy pastored. My husband and I made arrangements to attend. When we drove up to the church, we could not get in. White people were setting the cars of those inside the meeting on fire and breaking the windows in the automobiles. They were throwing gas bombs that exploded in the streets. Reverend King tried to talk to those outside. The National Guard had been called out and were around the church. However, I could not tell who the troops were for. Robert and I decided to leave. As we were driving away, I saw a car passing the church. An object was thrown at it, struck the moving vehicle, and broke one of the windows.

"Let's get away from here," I told my husband.

We were at a stop light. Robert said: "The light is red."

"You keep driving," I demanded politely.

My husband ran the red and we went home.

We learned the next day that those in the church had to stay there all night.

One of the most insightful strategies developed by the movement's leadership was to purchase vehicles to transport the bus boycotters. Some of the monies donated to the movement were used to help procure station wagons. No car dealer in Montgomery would sell vehicles to the movement. The reasoning of local whites was that if the bus boycotters were forced to walk or coordinate rides all would become frustrated in time and return to the city buses.

Mr. E. D. Nixon made arrangements to acquire the first station wagon. Mr. Nixon was a sleeping car porter. He knew people and had connections in several states. The first station wagon came from Cincinnati. I became the archivist at Alabama State College Library and worked there for many years. All of Mr. Nixon's papers are housed there. He used to come around often and visit.

One day he showed me a photograph. He pointed to himself and asked: "Do you know who that is?"

"Yes, that's you."

He pointed to a white gentleman in the picture and asked: "Can you see what that man is holding out to me."

"Yes, some keys," I answered correctly.

It was then that Mr. Nixon explained to me that he arranged to procure the first station wagon for the movement. He did not tell me who drove the car to Montgomery. Many other station wagons were purchased later from dealers closer to Montgomery. One can secure photographs from the bus boycott era and see all of the station wagons with the names of churches on the sides.

Mr. Nixon was a prime mover in the community and in the movement. Reverend King and Mrs. Parks have received most of the credit and accolades. However, I feel, as many others do, that Mr. Nixon has not been accorded the proper recognition due him. A plaque or marker has been placed in front of his home, but this is hardly indicative of his efforts. Several persons who did far less than Mr. Nixon have received greater honors. Honoring him is not so important, but honor should be extended to whom honor is due.

Long before Reverend King came to town Mr. Nixon was already at work. He brought Reverend Adam Clayton Powell to Montgomery to speak to the Black community in the late 1940s. Somehow Mr. Nixon secured the auditorium at Alabama State College for the event. Many of the teachers at the College were afraid to go to the program and hear Reverend Powell's address. I was there and participated on the program. I either introduced the speaker or explained the purpose of the program. That was over forty years ago and I cannot recall which function was assigned to me. A few teachers in the city were present. Most looked at me as if I were crazy. They thought I was going to lose my job.

As the decades passed, the older E. D. Nixon felt that he had been pushed underneath the bridge of history and his labors tossed in the dark tunnel of time. Years after the Montgomery Bus Boycott and other related events the Southern Christian Leadership Conference (SCLC) had a large meeting in Montgomery. I do not recall where the gathering was held. It was not at Dexter. Mr. Nixon did not have a seat on the platform with the other leaders. He came to my office afterward. I watched the old warrior cry. His tears moved me. He explained: "I entered and took a seat in the audience. I did not go near the front. I did not want anyone to think I desired a seat with the rest of the dignitaries."

Mr. Nixon was a tall robust man. Everyone present had to notice him when he entered and they must have noticed that he was not sitting with the other fighters for freedom, justice, and equality. He told me while sobbing: "When Reverend Abernathy got up to make remarks he said, 'Brother Nix, come on up here. I'll get a chair for you'. Reverend Abernathy insisted so I went up."

Mr. Nixon went to his grave a hurt man. This I know. He visited the archive section almost weekly and always took time to talk with me. He was not bitter, but hurt. It is possible to have the latter without the former.

I hated to see Reverend King leave our community. He did something for Montgomery that was needed. As Reverend King used to put it: "I am trying to bring the Ph.D.s and no Ds together. Before this matter is resolved the Ph.D.s will have to walk with the no Ds."

Such statements were precipitated by the professional Black people approaching Reverend King and reminding him of who they were and that the Black professionals and the domestics were on different levels. Admittedly before Reverend King came to town we had a clannish Black group in Montgomery. Some Black folk simply did not associate with others. However, in order to do what Reverend King accomplished, a general coming together of the race was necessary.

Reverend King desired that the professional and college-trained individuals assume their rightful places in the movement. These classes did not step forward as readily as he desired. Many of the professional people were afraid.

In later years Reverend King began to make public speeches about longevity having its place and how he would like to live a long life. However, I heard him make statements along these lines more than a decade before.

Upon learning that he had been assassinated, the words Reverend King uttered that morning at the parsonage after talking to the mean man rung in my head. I could clearly hear him saying:

"Before it is over someone will lose his life. It could be me. But I'm going on."

He did go on. Reverend King went to the end.

Birthday club
    ↳ social cohesion that
brought together professional r
domestic members of the
congregation.

Deacon Robert Williams

I was born and reared in Fayette County, Tennessee. I came from Memphis to Montgomery. The opportunity for educational advancement brought me to Alabama State College. I came to Dexter Avenue Baptist Church when Dr. Vernon Johns was the pastor. Dr. Johns married me and a beautiful young lady who had grown up in Dexter named Bertha Pleasant.

I was a member of Dexter only a few years before Reverend King came. I worked out of town and was away most of the time. I coached all four primary sports. Basketball, however, was my great love.

My love for sports led me to attend local sporting events when possible. I was at a football game at Alabama State College and observed a distinguished-looking young gentleman. I asked someone: "Who is that young man?"

"That's the new pastor of Dexter Avenue Baptist Church."

This was the first time I saw Reverend King.

My wife has provided most of our recollections of Reverend King. In addition to what she has already said, I was one of the men who stood guard at the parsonage. The local environment became very threatening to Reverend King.

One night I had a weapon, but there was nothing to it. It was more of a show for me than anything else. I did not have a liking for guns and the weapon was not mine. The person I relieved handed it to me. I remained there that night until Reverend King came home around 11:30 p.m. Bertha and I only lived a short distance from the parsonage. I do not think he knew I had a weapon

Reverend King knew how to get people off of his back. One episode in particular stands out in my mind. I do not recall all of the details. But something came up along the rumor line. There were often rumors circulating about Reverend King. Many of them were probably designed to weaken his influence. There were rumors such as him stealing or misappropriating monies from the movement. A charge of this nature was leveled on this particular occasion. Revered King's only response was: "Well, my father told me these things would happen."

He did not pursue the matter.

I was sad to see Reverend King leave our community. He had done so much. On the other hand, I was glad for what he was going to do for the race and for humanity. We all knew he would do greater things.

Deacon John Feagin, Sr.

I attended a mass meeting at Beulah Baptist Church in Montgomery during the period of the bus boycott. Reverend King was the speaker that evening. I was a student at Alabama State College. It was on this occasion that he made his initial but lasting impression on me. He delivered a very inspiring speech that night.

I was greatly impressed with Reverend King's leadership during the bus boycott.

The bus boycott was successfully prosecuted. I think a great deal of the success has to be attributed to the Governor of Alabama at the time and the white establishment in general. The establishment would not yield to the demands of Black residents. If the establishment had yielded within the first three or four months of the bus boycott and given all that was demanded, I do not think Black people would have pressed as hard as they did. It was the refusal of the white establishment to give in that made those boycotting the bus system so determined. Had the whites given in it would have taken away some of our steam and drive.

Shortly after the bus boycott commenced, I think Reverend King's vision expanded. I felt that things were really going to change, especially after the bus boycott ended. Many people felt, since we had taken on the bus system and won, we could take on more and be equally successful.

I started attending Dexter Avenue Baptist Church. I was regular in attendance during my college years.

In his sermons and casual conversations, Reverend King had a chilling effect on his listeners. Reverend King was a real down-to-earth person and was not spoiled by his academic achievements and abilities. He was an assured and in-charge person with a tremendous sense of humor.

Reverend King was able to bridge the imaginary generation gap. He was very comfortable with all groups. He constantly demonstrated tolerance, exhibited wisdom, restraint, and understanding regarding the problems of adults. These qualities were evident in his work with the Dexter flock which had the usual disagreements and concerns of a church body. After a meeting, there was always the shaking of hands, unforgettable laughter, and pats on our backs by Dr. King. He was concerned about the growth and spiritual development of Dexter Avenue Baptist Church from the day of his arrival.

Reverend King enjoyed good Southern food. One of his favorite homes to dine in was that of Mrs. Sally Madison on Grove Street. Mrs. Madison and I were in the August Month Club.

I officially united with Dexter in 1960. After getting married, my wife, Lurlene, joined Dexter. The one regret in my acquaintance with Reverend King is that Lurlene and I did not ask him to perform our marriage.

Reverend King left Dexter Avenue Baptist Church and Montgomery in January 1960. Several weeks before his departure Lurlene and I stopped by to visit with him in the pastor's study at the church. During this visit, I presented Reverend King a Black working man that I had sculpted for him. He expressed his appreciation and said: "I will always treasure this."

I was an art teacher at Carver High School in Montgomery, where I taught for thirty-four years. Lurlene was also an educator. While in Reverend King's office that day shortly before his departure from Montgomery, Lurlene and I asked Reverend King his feelings and insights regarding integration in the public schools. My wife and I were young educators and really wanted to hear what he thought. Reverend King's reply went along this line: "I favor integration on buses and in all areas of public accommodation and travel. I am for equality. However, I think integration in our public schools is different. In that setting you are dealing with one of the most important assets of an individual—the mind. White people view Black people as inferior. A large percentage of them have a very low opinion of our race. People with such a low view of the Black race cannot be given free reign and put in charge of the intellectual care and development of our boys and girls." He went on to say: "I don't see school integration successfully happening right now and being beneficial. I think the school system will have a problem. It will be disastrous. Training will be necessary. White educators especially will need training in how to deal with Black children. They will have to come to grips with their prejudices. Without such training I don't think it will work. Love, tolerance, and respect on the part of white people and Black people are mandatory. If integration is to work in the public schools, it will have to be a gradual process."

Reverend King indicated that the sons and daughters of Black lawyers, physicians, educators, and other professionals would do well academically and rise up to the occasion.

His great concern was for the vast population of poor Black boys and girls in an integrated academic setting. It was the poor people whom he had courageously led. It was the domestics and common laborers who rode the buses in Montgomery. The bus boycott was basically their struggle. Reverend King had sympathy for this class. Reverend King felt that in view of the attitude of white teachers and the deep prejudices they would bring to the classroom environment the Black race would lose a large number of potential leaders, as well as good solid boys and girls who needed only a small amount of encouragement to forge ahead and make significant accomplishments and contributions. White teachers were not likely to give that extra push and encouragement to Black boys and girls.

In retrospect, I am convinced of the correctness of Reverend King's reasoning. He was right.

Many of the Black boys and girls who were in the first wave of integration suffered immensely. These boys and girls were just thrown into the setting without any preparation on the part of administrators, teachers, parents, or any other group. The Black boys and girls in this initial wave of integration faced so many discouraging episodes until learning lost its appeal. Many of them had a vast amount of potential and were good students prior to integration. It is the children of this class and their grandchildren with whom we are having so many problems today.

After integration was instituted, we discovered that many white teachers in the State of Alabama did not hold degrees from any institution of higher learning. In contrast, the Black teachers held degrees, and many had earned degrees above the bachelor status.

After the death of Dr. King, I drew a mural on one side of the wall in the lower level of the church. I thought some lasting visible expression to our former pastor should be a part of the church. Dr. Zelia Evans was responsible for procuring the needed funds from the church for the project. The painting depicts in various scenes the story of the struggle from the commencement of the bus boycott until the death of Reverend King.

Mr. Frank Pollard

Reverend Pollard preceded Reverend Vernon Johns as the pastor of Dexter Avenue Baptist Church. Reverend Pollard was my father's uncle. We just called him Uncle Bob.

I first saw Reverend King when he came to Dexter as a candidate for the pulpit. Everyone in the congregation was impressed with him from day one.

After Reverend King had been the pastor for a while, events now well known transpired. After things had been in progress for sometime, an element in the church began to express some concern. This group asserted that perhaps Reverend King was not right for Dexter.

President Trenholm was the head of Alabama State College and a member of Dexter. President Trenholm said after events started to happen: "God has sent this man to lead Dexter and it's time for a change."

Dr. Trenholm cared about the students. He would not allow them to be dismissed because they could not pay their fees. He reviewed each student's schedule and signed it himself. Dr. Trenholm was concerned about the future of the students and the kind of America in which they would live. He had the utmost respect for Reverend King.

Governor Patterson wanted many of the King supporters who worked at Alabama State College removed. Dr. Trenholm did not respond as swiftly in every instance as the governor demanded or desired. In the end, Governor Patterson terminated Dr. Trenholm. The latter became ill and took a leave of absence, but the governor's intention was executed. A successor to Dr. Trenholm was named.

Dr. Trenholm, to the end of his administration, believed in Reverend King and the position for which his pastor stood.

Very early many local Black people saw the lasting impact of Reverend King's work. Some Black people wanted Reverend King to turn around. The late Mr. P. M. Blair, a member of Dexter, owned a cleaning business. I was at his establishment one day and he said to me: "Reverend King is not going to turn around. He is too far out there now. He will be the greatest man to live in the next one hundred years."

After the successful completion of the Montgomery Bus Boycott the movement escalated. Mrs. Jo Ann Robinson said at the MIA office one day: "There is no better time to get Black people registered and Alabama on the move."

Voter Registration became a focal point.

As the leader of the movement, Reverend King's life was in jeopardy. His wife and children at the time were also potential targets. One home in which the Kings and their children were given sanctuary was at the residence of Mrs. Mary Lewis Morgan on Mt. Meigs Road in Montgomery. She was a school teacher and worked at Daisy Lawrence School on Beach Street. Mrs. Morgan kept the children often. The children were very small at the time. Both King and Abernathy were fond of Mrs. Morgan.

The Kings were also given sanctuary in other homes in the community.

Pressure increasingly mounted against Reverend King. It came from the white establishment, but indirectly. Parishioners of Dexter Avenue Baptist Church started pressuring the pastor. Many members worked in the public school system. They owned big-ticket items for which they had to make payments—cars, houses, and such. These people could not afford to be terminated from their jobs. If they had been terminated, their homes, vehicles, and other symbols of success would have been snatched from them. The white establishment obviously held over some individuals' heads the possibility of great material loss.

It is my contention that Reverend King was not all that he wanted to be. I am convinced that Reverend King held back on account of Dexter and did not go full speed ahead. He wanted Dexter and all of the members to be more out front. He wanted his church to be the model church for America and take the lead in the struggle and make a difference.

Reverend King felt this pressure from the inside. I noticed a change in his preaching during the latter period of his pastorate. He became more direct in his preaching. His disappointment was apparent. He felt the church should have been more involved.

I had lunch with Reverend King one day at the State Office Building adjacent to the church. This was not a planned luncheon. We just happened to be in the building at the same time.

He said: "Frank, it's time for me to move on. I have done all they [the church] will allow me to do."

I said: "Dr. King, you have to go where God leads you, but I don't want you to leave."

This was before Reverend King announced publicly that he was leaving.

I believe to this day that Reverend King did not want to leave Montgomery. He had accomplished so much here. His work in Montgomery had become a model for other cities. He departed Montgomery because there were not that many viable options available. The inside forces that were laboring against him probably helped Reverend King reach a decision that he would not have arrived at under ordinary circumstances.

However, Reverend King was no ordinary person. He was one of the greatest men who has ever lived or will live.

Deacon William B. Gary

I came to Alabama State College in the fall of 1953. I met Reverend King in 1954. I played football for the college. The football coach was a Congregationalist and attended a church of his denomination not far from the campus. It was his practice to carry the players to church on Sunday with him. There was also a vespers service on the campus at 3:00 p.m. on Sunday which all had to attend. That is how it was back then.

I was Baptist and explained to the coach that I wanted to attend a church of my denomination. That is how I started attending Dexter Avenue Baptist Church.

When Reverend King was called to be the pastor of Dexter Avenue Baptist Church, I continued to attend. He was a good preacher. His sermons were comparable to those heard in a regular Baptist church on Sunday mornings. Worshippers were urged to live good lives, do right, and love God.

I lived in a dormitory with some other students who attended Dexter Avenue Baptist Church over the years. John Porter, Harold Carter, and T. Y. Rogers were all brothers of Alpha Phi Alpha Fraternity, Inc., and entered the ministry. Reverend King had a great influence on each. They wanted me to become an Alpha, but most of the men in my hometown belonged to Kappa Alpha Psi Fraternity. I pledged the latter fraternity.

John Porter used to be Reverend King's assistant. I used to go and hear my friend deliver the Sunday sermon when the opportunity was extended to him.

After the commencement of the bus boycott, the organization purchased station wagons so the protesters could be transported to and from work. The station wagons were also used to transport members to and from church. I drove for Dexter.

I drove people to and from Sunday School, worship service, Baptist Training Union, which was held on Sunday afternoon, mid-week service, conventions, and other gatherings. The ladies of the church were especially busy during those years and kept me behind the steering wheel going here and there.

I was paid four dollars a week. There was a student at Alabama State College younger than I. His name was Clarence Bozeman. In later years he started driving the station wagon. It allowed him to earn some money as a student. When Clarence went home at Christmas recess and during the summer, I resumed my old duties.

Once the bus boycott was in effect it was unsafe to walk the streets at night. Many fun activities had to cease. For example, my fraternity,

Kappa Alpha Psi, used to do some crazy things with the college men who were pledging. Those pledging would be instructed to walk at night from Alabama State College campus to Saint Jude School on Fairview Avenue, which was about five miles away. There they would find a red and white rock with a note under it. The note might have read: "Go to First Baptist Church." Reverend Ralph Abernathy was the pastor there and a fraternity brother. At First Baptist Church someone might have told them to go to Ross-Clayton Funeral Home. There was a brother who worked at that establishment.

Being out at night became a hazard. White people would take Black people in their custody and perform violent acts against them or do anything to strike fear in the Black population at large.

Many of us on the campus did a few mischievous acts also. We used to hide behind bushes at night. When white people drove in the vicinity of Jackson Street, we would assault their vehicles with rocks.

There is no doubt that Reverend King prevented a riot the night the church parsonage was bombed. There were hundreds and hundreds of people standing in the yard of the parsonage. Reverend King urged them to remain calm and return to their homes. Most of the establishments in the vicinity of Jackson and High Streets were Black-owned.

One night we heard that Hutchinson Street Baptist Church had been bombed. It was located about two blocks from the campus. Many of us rushed over to see how we could assist.

Later we heard that the home of Reverend Abernathy had been bombed. In like manner, many of us ran to his home. However, there was no truth to this story.

I attended mass meetings. They were very exciting. Many times people stood outside and listened because there was no room in the church. There was always good preaching, singing, and praying. The preachers gave the people a lot of fire. Black folk basically preached, prayed, and sang their way through the bus boycott and the movement.

In 1958, I became a member of Dexter and joined the choir. It was different in those days. There were many professional men and women in the choir. If one used bad grammar, he or she was corrected. One had to sound out his or her words. The highest comportment was expected. The choir sang anthems primarily.

Dexter had numerous professional people in its membership. Many of the Black professionals supported the movement undercover by giving financial support. It was not all poor Black people whom Reverend King rallied and who marched with him.

Reverend King was an excellent pastor, preacher and orator. However, I had one major frustration during the period of the movement. My irritation centered around the crowd that came to Dexter Avenue Baptist Church. The church would be filled to capacity on Sunday morning. There was standing room only. However, when Reverend King was not scheduled to preach the people would come in much smaller numbers. It appeared as if they were coming to church for the wrong reason. Many of them were coming for no other reason than because of Reverend King, his presence, and personality. He was saying what the people felt and wanted to hear. His words were timely and true; nevertheless that did not negate what was happening.

My contention is that if a person loves God and is committed to doing the will of God he or she will be in church on Sunday regardless of who is preaching.

I felt that Dexter needed a more stable, well-nurtured band of believers, who had a local flavor, and were believers committed to the cause of Christ. This could not have been achieved under the auspices of the movement. Reverend King did not use the movement as an avenue for church growth. Events just ended up that way. Reverend King was the head of the movement as well as a local pastor and national figure, so people naturally flocked to Dexter. I would have been far more satisfied had the growth of the church been centered around Reverend King's preaching and pastoral leadership. When Reverend King came to Dexter, that was probably his aim. He did not come with the intention to lead a movement.

In light of the irritation I had with the crowd situation, I welcomed Reverend King's departure. He was an excellent preacher and orator, and had superb pastoral skills; however, I wanted to see the church return to a more stable fundamental footing under the leadership of a pastor whose personality was not so prominent. I wanted people to come and join Dexter based on a higher principle. Reverend King definitely preached a social gospel during the movement.

Reverend King resigned as pastor of Dexter Avenue Baptist Church. Soon thereafter one could enter the sanctuary and find a seat any time. The need to arrive early for worship in order to get a seat was over. Reverend King's departure from Dexter and that of the crowd were almost simultaneous.

I have a photograph at home of myself and Reverend King. Shortly before his assassination he returned to Dexter to preach. As was his custom, he walked to the rear of the church following the sermon to shake the hand of each parishioner leaving the sanctuary. A photographer took a photograph of myself and my former pastor. I was later given a copy of the picture. It is proudly displayed in my home.

After being ordained a deacon, I gave up my driving duties. Thirty-one years elapsed between the time I started and my resignation.

Mrs. Minnie Woods-Dixon

I started attending Dexter Avenue Baptist Church with my husband. He was the late Mr. Edward Woods, Sr. Edward grew up in Dexter.

I was led to join Dexter in 1954. I made my desire known to Reverend King to be baptized. Several months elapsed before my baptism took place. Reverend King was not the problem. I was afraid of the water. Reverend King telephoned me several times and inquired about my intentions. Each time I assured him that I still wanted to be baptized, but was afraid. He was very understanding. Reverend King assured me repeatedly in his several telephone calls that everything would be just fine. He made comforting statements such as: "Don't be afraid. It will be alright."

I kept coming up with excuses. Several months passed before I acquired enough nerve to do it.

I joined the Young Matrons Club. That was an exciting group. We met and made plans for the church.

The planning sessions I really enjoyed were those regarding Vacation Bible School. It was always held during the summer. I was one of the Vacation Bible School teachers. I had a lot of fun working with the children.

When Vacation Bible School was in session, Reverend King came by every day near the closing hour to visit the boys and girls. He acted like a school principal. He was concerned about the children and their spiritual development.

"How was the day?" he would ask them.

They would respond to the pastor.

During his daily visits, Reverend King would ask the boys and girls a few biblical questions about the day's lesson to see how much they had learned and retained. They would raise their hands hoping to be called upon or yell out answers. Reverend King worked well with children.

It was a joy to have known Reverend King. He was warm and friendly. A person was never afraid to talk to him. He made you feel comfortable. Reverend King was very personable.

His preaching was so touching. Everyone could understand him. Some ministers preach sermons and people go away not knowing or understanding what was said. Soon people started coming from all around to hear Reverend King. He was a very inspiring minister.

When around Reverend King, one got a certain feeling. One got the feeling that he was a godly man. You could just feel it. Reverend King was a great pastor to the congregation. Babies are not baptized in the

Baptist church. The denomination embraces believers' baptism. However, a baby can be dedicated to the Lord. Reverend King dedicated our daughter, Valerie.

Reverend King left Montgomery in January 1960. Our son, Edward, Jr., was born on 4 October 1960. Reverend King returned to Montgomery shortly after the birth of Edward. My husband and I asked Reverend King to dedicate the baby. He honored our request and dedicated Edward to the Lord.

King: The Community Pastor

Mrs. Johnnie R. Carr

Reverend King was the first president of the Montgomery Improvement Association (MIA). I am the fifth head executive and the only female to hold the position of president.

Long before the MIA came into existence there was political activity in Montgomery within the Black community. Mr. Rufus Lewis labored unendingly to get members of the race registered so we could participate in the political process. He had a mimeograph machine and used to run off the test that people had to pass before they could register.

I worked for a Black-owned company called Atlanta Life Insurance. When our agents were in the field, they talked to Black people about registering.

We used to hold training sessions in the company's building. Churches gave us access and when necessary we gathered in homes. When we felt candidates were ready to pass the written test, they were carried to the courthouse to take the exam. The test was given between 8:00 a.m. and 4:00 p.m. Of course, most Black people were at work during those hours. That was a part of the strategy to keep Black people out of the process.

I took the exam and passed in 1946. Seven persons were to go that morning. Four persons could not go.

After learning I had passed the test, I was told that I owed $21.00 cumulative poll-tax. I did not have $21.00. Mr. Burch was the manager of the insurance company where I worked. When he discovered I had passed the test, but did not have the $21.00, he called me and said: "Johnnie, come get the money and take it down there before they change their minds."

I paid $1.50 poll-tax each year thereafter until the tax was abolished.

The League of Women Voters worked to abolish the poll-tax. I was in this organization also.

I was a member of the local chapter of the NAACP. Mr. E. D. Nixon was the president. He was an outspoken person, but not violent. The membership reached the point where a more temperate leader was desired. A gentleman named Mr. T. T. Allen was nominated to run against Mr. Nixon. People were canvassed to come and vote for Mr. Allen. The meeting was held at Holt Street Baptist Church. I was the secretary. When all of Mr. Nixon's community accomplishments were enumerated and his labors on behalf of the race highlighted, practically all of the people voted for him. Mr. Nixon remained in office.

Indeed Mr. Nixon had done much for the Black community. He was a Pullman porter and knew many people across the land. Once Mr. Nixon sought to accomplish a feat in Montgomery and faced obstacles. He knew Mrs. Eleanor Roosevelt. She personally threw her influence behind Mr. Nixon and he achieved his goal.

I had a problem once near my house. The city was dumping unwanted waste near Hall Street where I lived. Flies gravitated to the dumping ground. I could hardly cook in my kitchen on some hot summer days because of the flies. I contacted Mr. Nixon. He gave me the name of a white attorney in Montgomery.

"Tell him I gave you his name," Mr. Nixon said over the phone.

The attorney took my case. We successfully sued the city to have the dumping ground relocated.

I first saw Reverend King in Montgomery on a Sunday afternoon. Robert Nesbitt, Sr., who was a deacon at Dexter Avenue Baptist Church, brought young Reverend King to Metropolitan United Methodist Church on Jefferson Davis Avenue. We were having an NAACP meeting. Reverend King was not on to speak or anything. He was new in town and was being presented at the monthly meeting.

Reverend King was given the opportunity to make remarks. He stood before the body and began to address the audience. I was seated next to Mrs. Rosa Parks. As Reverend King spoke, I looked at my friend and said to her: "Rosa, he is something else."

Everybody in attendance that Sunday afternoon concluded that Reverend King was different. There was something about him. I could not put it in words back in 1954 and cannot adequately state it forty years later.

After this meeting, I saw Reverend King at other functions in the community. These were mostly political events. Reverend King had a bent toward political activity and wanted to help redress the wrongs faced by the Black community.

Mrs. Parks and I were only two of a few females who attended the NAACP meetings. She was the secretary and I worked with the Youth Council. Some years the positions were reversed. I was elected secretary and she was in charge of the youth.

After Reverend King came to Dexter and began to move about in the community, members of the local chapter of the NAACP again expressed the desire to have a new president. It rained on the day the election was to be held. Mr. E. D. Nixon remained president. The membership had its eyes on Reverend Abernathy or Reverend King. The latter was the preference.

My friend, Rosa, was arrested for occupying the wrong seat on a Montgomery city bus. The world knows what happened and how Reverend King became the president of the MIA.

Reverend King was articulate and could be a voice for *all* the Black residents of Montgomery. His educational attainment did not create a barrier between himself and the common people. He spoke their language and felt their pain. Moreover, he wanted to help do something about it.

Reverend King was elected president of the MIA, but he never dominated any situation. Other ministers always spoke at the mass meetings and participated in other ways. Reverend King never tried to lift himself up. One never got the feeling that he felt it was his movement. He was a meek man, but a staunch leader.

Everybody related to him and he to everybody. Reverend King loved everybody. He had a special fondness for old ladies and little babies.

The bus boycott continued and the people were determined to see it through. I had a car and did not ride the bus. However, if I or my husband, Arlam Carr, Sr., was off to a certain side of town, it was a common practice to drive by the Posey Parking Lot and pick up passengers. For example, if I was going to the west side of Montgomery, I would stop by and have it announced that I was going to that area of town and three or four riders were welcomed.

My son, Arlam, Jr., as were many boys and girls at the time, was equally excited about what was going on. If we were going somewhere and he saw a Black person along the street or on a side street that I did not see, he would alert me. "Mama, there is somebody walking."

I would turn around and inquire whether the person needed a ride.

One of the most memorable scenes from the period of the bus boycott occurred one day while I was driving on Decatur Street. I saw many domestics walking to the Cloverdale section where most of them worked. They were laughing and talking. The most moving thing about it all was that it was raining cats and dogs that day. The women were strolling as if they were walking in God's sunshine. The rain belonged to God also.

The bus boycott had been going on for sometime and successfully. However, I became concerned after noticing a trend at several mass meetings. All of the ministers were usually present, together with the regular band of supporters. I went by the home of my old friend and co-civic worker E. D. Nixon one day. I used to call him Nix.

"Nix, I've been missing you at the meetings," I stated, and not wasting any time or words I asked: "What's going on? What's the matter?"

"Well, Johnnie," he commenced, "I've been pulling chestnuts out of the fire for the niggers in this town down through the years. Now everything is KING, KING, KING." He went on to say with a degree of resentment in his voice: "When I enter a meeting now, the people hardly recognize me. As soon as Reverend and Mrs. King come in, the people try to take the roof off."

"Awww, Nix, you shouldn't feel like that," I consoled. "You've been a strong figure in this community. You have done just as much and in many cases more for our people in Montgomery than anyone." My words of consolation did not comfort my long-time friend.

Reverend King never courted the success or popularity accorded him. Between the late 1940s and 1960 there were two distinct periods in Montgomery. They were the pre-King era (before Martin Luther King, Jr., came to Montgomery) and the King era. The latter was the period during which he resided in Montgomery, 1954-1960. Mr. Nixon was one of the dominant personalities in the Black community during the pre-King period. Mr. Nixon also was the prime mover in rallying the preachers and leaders of the Black community after Rosa's arrest. It was Mr. Nixon who got Rosa out of jail. He was basically responsible for getting the station wagons that were purchased to transport the bus boycotters. The bus boycott was a people's effort and they fully embraced Reverend King as their leader. Mr. Nixon was not pushed aside and Reverend King had the utmost respect for him. I think Brother Nixon took it all personally and read more into matters than was really there. He stopped coming to the meetings and separated himself.

My consolation is in knowing that E. D. Nixon's name will never stop being mentioned whenever people talk about Montgomery from the 1940s to 1955/56.

The bus boycott was a complete success. The movement grew and other issues were addressed. Black people began demonstrating and demanding their civil rights. Reverend King's philosophy was that of non-violence, which he borrowed from Gandhi.

Many citizens in Montgomery, preachers included, found that concept very difficult to embrace. People supported Reverend King and his call for justice from the white establishment. However, many were not willing to be beaten, bitten by dogs, and sprayed by water hoses. Their level of tolerance was not that high. Reverend King taught that persons willing to demonstrate had to train themselves to think and act a certain way. The key was not to become angry. Reverend King used to say: "If ever a person makes you angry, you are defeated. If you hold your temper, you can win."

Those who desired to participate in the marches were prohibited from having anything on their person that could be used as a weapon. Women could not have a pin in their hats. Men accustomed to carrying small pocket knives were to leave them at home. The reasoning was that if anyone became angry he or she would use the first item available as a weapon.

In spite of this sound reasoning, many persons were unwilling to buy into the idea. Initially people said things such as: "If I have to do things that way, count me out. If someone hits me or spits on me, I will strike back."

A large number of Black people, and the whites who joined in, finally saw the wisdom of Reverend King's idea.

Reverend King was a model leader. Whenever there was a march, he was not in a hotel room relaxing. He never sent the troops to the front line alone. The pictures readers see in books and magazines from that era with Reverend King in front of all the other marchers were not staged. Reverend King always went with us. Nothing deterred him. He was beaten, jailed, and ill-treated in many other ways, but he held to the position of non-violent protest.

This was the main weapon in his arsenal. White southerners expected King supporters to become violent in time. They thought the patience of Black people would wear thin. It never occurred to the white establishment that members of the oppressed race would conduct themselves in a dignified manner indefinitely. They consistently beat, jailed, and put the dogs on us, hoping to drive the protesters to violence. Had the Black protesters turned violent that would have ended the movement. We would have never been able to stand up against the weapons and artillery possessed by the ruling class. Reverend King's non-violent strategy took the whites by surprise. They had no alternate plan to defeat or turn us back. I heard the former mayor of Selma, Alabama, say in later years that he could not understand the non-violent tactic.

"We beat them and everything else," the mayor said in retrospect, "but the people would not turn violent. I could not understand it then, but I see now," he confessed.

Reverend King left Montgomery in 1960. Several persons served as president of the MIA. In 1967 I became the fifth president. I am still the executive head and the only female to ever occupy the position.

Events related to the movement brought Reverend King back to Montgomery several times in the following years. Once he was invited to Montgomery to speak on a special occasion on a Sunday afternoon. It was shortly after the assassination of President John F. Kennedy. An episode took place and vintage King emerged.

I do not recall the special event for which Reverend King had been invited back to speak. He had to preach in Atlanta that Sunday morning, then catch an afternoon flight to Montgomery. Like many others, I was delighted with the idea of him being among us again for just a few hours. Mrs. Irene West, Mrs. Erna Dungee Allen and I were appointed to pick Reverend King up from the Montgomery Airport. Mrs. Allen was the driver. Near the airport I observed three white men. Something came over me. I did not feel good about them, though they did not immediately do anything to suggest trouble.

"Did you all see those three men back there?" I asked as we rode into the airport parking lot.

"No," the other ladies replied. "What men?"

"I saw three men back there who looked suspicious."

I could not provide any other tangible evidence to support my feelings. The subject was dropped.

We parked and went into the terminal area. After being inside for a few minutes, Mrs. Allen was paged. She went to the pager and returned, explaining: "Reverend King has been delayed in Atlanta. He missed his flight and will be on the next plane to Montgomery. We will stay here and wait for him?"

Montgomery had a very small airport. It was a typical small town facility. Airplanes parked almost at the door. Travelers exited their aircraft and walked right into the terminal.

The initial flight that Reverend King was supposed to be on landed. The passengers got off and started moving toward the entrance. The three men I saw earlier were walking abreast toward the entrance where Reverend King was to enter had he been on the aircraft.

"There are the three men I was talking about," I whispered to Irene and Erna, having to say no more.

We watched them. The men eyed all of the passengers. The plane was empty. Reverend King did not get off. The three turned and walked hurriedly from the arrival area.

Mrs. West went and made a telephone call. She explained that something suspicious was going on at the airport. Within twenty to thirty minutes five or six cars arrived carrying King supporters.

The later plane that Reverend King was on arrived. He walked inside smiling as always. The fifteen or so persons who had gathered at the airport immediately surrounded him. Someone said: "Reverend, you stay in the middle. Something did not seem right out here earlier."

We walked down the corridor with Reverend King in our midst. He lifted the left coat lapel with his left thumb and did the same with the right lapel.

"This is great," he said smiling and walking. "This is great."

We walked a little further. Suddenly Reverend King caught himself and reminded those of us around him: "You know President Kennedy had the Secret Service, the Highway Patrol, State Police, body guards, and a host of others as protectors; but they still got to him. You are not going before your time."

Reverend King knew that it was not yet his time. However, I am convinced he knew his time was limited. In spite of that, he did not turn back and for that the world is eternally indebted to him.

We had a fine program that afternoon.

I also became a board member of the Southern Christian Leadership Conference in 1967. I discovered that Reverend King was still fighting the battle of trying to convince ministers that non-violent protest was a viable option. It had been practiced now for several years. I heard ministers say to him: "Doctor, I will support you and give you funds for the cause, but this thing of not retaliating I cannot buy into."

There was a radical element within the Black community in the late 1960s. This element felt that violence was the answer and they were gaining sympathizers.

The SCLC held a board meeting in Washington, D.C., in 1968. Reverend King was the speaker. Prior to addressing the SCLC he spoke with three other groups around the city.

When Reverend King gave his address to the SCLC body, Bobby Seale, Stokely Carmichael and other known radicals were present. Reverend King talked about non-violent protest and its benefits. The radical element listened for a while. Then the leader stood up and tapped each member of his group on the shoulder. When all were on their feet, the leader started walking toward the door. The others followed. They were trying to humiliate the speaker. Reverend King continued with his speech. He never pushed aside the main agenda to entertain petty issues. I broke down and cried. I did not cry for Reverend King's sake. I cried for the radical element who could not see the beauty of Reverend King's concept.

Violence breeds violence. There is no doubt in my mind that had Black people turned violent during the movement they would have been annihilated. The same holds true today.

Convincing enough people to try the non-violent approach was the crowning genius of Reverend King's work. I am glad that heaven allowed me to be a participant in the movement and work with Reverend King.

Mrs. Dorothy Calhoun

I grew up in Salitpa, which is located in Clarke County, Alabama. Clarke County had white physicians, white cabs, and such and Black people made use of them. However, Salitpa was basically segregated.

I left home in the summer of 1953 to attend Alabama State College. I arrived in Montgomery on a Greyhound bus. After claiming my belongings at the bus terminal, I stepped outside of the station and flagged a cab to take me to the campus. I hailed a white cab, which was the first one in view. The driver stopped and told me I had to get a Black taxi to transport me to the campus. This was my welcome to Montgomery.

The system and rules in Montgomery were horrible. I grew tired of staring at empty seats on the bus that I could not sit in. I recall occasions when the bus was filled with Black people, but the four seats across the front of the bus could not be occupied. Black riders had to stand. Standing and seeing those reserved unoccupied seats rubbed me worse than having to move for a white person.

There was always one episode that caused something to swell up in me. It was seeing old Black men and women, who could hardly move, deposit their money and while walking to the back door of the bus to get on the white driver would pull away.

I heard about the bus boycott. I was delighted with the news. I thought to myself—someone is finally going to try and straighten things out.

I first saw Dr. King at a mass meeting which was held at Hutchinson Street Baptist Church. This church was walking distance from the campus.

Forty years later I still remember that meeting. The church was filled to capacity. A little man commanded the attention of the audience. I was surprised at the small physical stature of Reverend King. He kept everybody on the edge of their seats. The people cheered him on. There was an indescribable intensity in his speech. Reverend King was saying what so many others felt, but did not have the boldness to say.

An awesome feeling seized me that evening. This was the first time I had been involved in anything with my race and the spirit of fear was absent. That was how I knew something special was happening. This was also the first time I had witnessed a majority of Black people following a member of their own race. Reverend King left no doubt that he was with the people and it was his intention to help remedy some of the wrongs systematically imposed upon the race.

Up to this stage fear had always been employed as a means of control by white people. It was always there. Black children were never intentionally taught fear, but it was there. No Black person in those days could tell you the first time he or she became conscious of his or her fear, but it was present.

The Black citizens of Montgomery were with Reverend King. Spies were usually in attendance at mass meetings and would report to white people what was going on. No one ever wanted to be labeled a spy. Whatever Reverend King said was gospel. If one did not agree, he or she did nothing to hinder.

White people held to the fear tactics and it worked. For example, even after the protest had been going on for a while some Black ministers refused to allow mass meetings to be held in their churches.

Other scare tactics were employed. Tickets for driving violations were frequently given out to Black motorists. Insurance companies canceled policies. Most of the Black people in the city were poor and did not have ready cash. They would charge items at local stores. In many cases, these charge accounts were suspended. All of these were methods of control. The people, however, would not yield or be turned back. They knew the race had a leader this time in the person of Reverend King.

Reverend King was authentic and simple. He did not manipulate the people, although it would have been very easy for him to have done so. The majority of the poor people had definitely put all of their eggs in his basket. Their cause was his cause. Reverend King stood for something good and righteous. His word was good. Prior to him, it had been a long time since a leader emerged upon whose word the people could rely. Before Reverend King's time, a Black leader would say one thing and two weeks later it was the opposite. White people would dangle a piece of candy before the individual or pay the person off.

Reverend King was not a politician. That enhanced his credibility. It was obvious that he was not heading the movement for self-glorification. The risks were too great for self-advancement. The Black people in Montgomery remained strong throughout the period of the boycott because Reverend King remained strong. If he had crumbled, the people would have also crumbled.

The bus boycott ended in December 1956. White people did not readily embrace the new seating arrangement on city buses. Though segregation on city buses was declared unconstitutional, efforts were made to keep Black people off via fear. It was still dangerous to ride.

In January 1957, I was pregnant with twins. My family was living in Sheridan Heights in North Montgomery. I was riding the Boylston bus one day. After getting off, I later learned that someone had shot through the window of that same bus as it was going back to town.

After the successful completion of the bus boycott, the movement began to gain momentum. Non-violence was Reverend King's theme. I believed in what he was doing, but I could not embrace the non-violent concept. I could not and would not take a lick from anyone. The idea of being struck with an object did not set well with me.

Lessons and instructions were provided on how to shield oneself from a blow. People were taught how to position themselves so as to curb the severity of a blow.

I knew in my heart, however, that the non-violent method was the only way to gain success. I knew if I had participated in the marches I would have been a problem for the movement.

However, Reverend King did not hold it against individuals because they would not march. In fact, he encouraged people not to participate if they felt their presence would do more harm than good. Many people supported the movement, but could not accept the idea of non-violence.

In retrospect, everyone now sees the wisdom of Reverend King's method.

Reverend King could not have planned anything comparable to what transpired in Montgomery and the South. He was a God-sent man. There has not been a leader like Reverend King and will not be another until God deems the time right.

Mr. Clarence Bozeman

I was a student at Alabama State College. One day I learned that one of the administrators, Dean Wesley, wanted to see me. Dean Wesley informed me that Reverend Martin King had asked him to identify a student to drive the station wagon for Dexter Avenue Baptist Church. The primary duty of the driver was to pick up elderly parishioners and children for Sunday school, and later on Sunday morning pick up individuals who wanted to come to worship service.

"Go to Reverend King's home on Jackson Street and he will give you more particulars," the dean said.

Jackson Street ended at the entrance to the college. I walked up Jackson Street to Reverend King's home. I rang the bell and he opened the door. I explained my presence and was invited inside. Reverend King began his interview:

"Do you have a driver's license?" "Yes sir." I replied.

"Do you have a clean record?"

"Yes, sir, I do."

"Are you bondable?"

"Yes, sir, I am."

It was as though I was applying for a high position in a distinguished firm or organization. On the other hand, I was doing just that. The church is a prestigious organization.

Being satisfied with my answers Reverend King told me what he expected of the driver.

"You will pick up the elderly and children for Sunday school and church service. I expect you to be a gentleman at all times toward the elderly and the children. If anything develops, direct all questions to myself or Deacon Robert Nesbitt, Sr."

My first drive was to Sunday school. My first passengers were Yolanda and Martin, III.

I was paid $6.00 a week. That was an excellent salary for a college student in the 1950s who only had to drive on Sundays. Deacon Robert Nesbitt used to pay me in quarters. I asked him to pay me in dollars. I wanted to go back to the campus and flash my money.

After I had been driving for a few weeks, police officers began to follow me each Sunday morning. I was always careful to come to a complete stop at each stop sign, stop at each red light, never go through a yellow light, and yield at the proper time. I drove with such care even before I started being followed.

One Sunday I came to a full stop. I felt the presence of the officers. Sure enough they were behind me. I was given a ticket. I had done nothing improper. I was given the ticket basically because of my association with Dexter Avenue Baptist Church, where Reverend King was the pastor.

I successfully made my rounds. After putting the passengers out at the church, I told Reverend King what happened.

"Do you want to fight it?"

"Yes, I do," I said unhesitatingly.

I felt the ticket was given to me without cause.

Reverend King pursued the matter. Nothing became of the incident. I did not have to pay the fine.

My driving duties gradually expanded beyond Sunday. I used to drive Mrs. King to visit her family in Marion, Alabama. I met her father, mother, and brother. They were a strong, independent, closely knit family.

Reverend King made it clear that he did not want me to drive Mrs. King any place after dark. He did not want her out after sundown. Her safety meant everything to him.

Once I had to drive Mrs. King to South Alabama. While in route, she needed to freshen up, but there was no place for Black travelers to stop. We saw a house and a Black family moving about the grounds. I pulled into the yard. I introduced Mrs. King and myself to the man. He recognized Mrs. King before she was introduced. Obviously the man had seen her in media photographs.

The man was frightened. That was immediately apparent. He probably lived on a white man's land and feared what might happen to him and his family if it was discovered that the wife of Martin Luther King, Jr., had been on the premises.

After Mrs. King freshened up, we journeyed on. She was moved by the man's fear of her.

"I wonder how many other people there are around Alabama who feel that way," she said, referring to the Black man whose place we had just left.

I drove Reverend King to many speaking engagements. I recall driving him to Tuskegee on several occasions. Once he addressed an audience of African students at Tuskegee Institute. On the other visits Reverend King preached at churches in the town of Tuskegee.

Reverend King talked much about religion. He stressed religion. I did not appreciate much of what I heard from Reverend King until I got older. Now much of what he said and taught has become the bedrock of my Christian faith.

When I drove Reverend King to various destinations, we would talk along the way. Two subjects dominated our conversation. They were religion and education. His conversations were never senseless chatter. He always said something meaningful.

Sometimes he would not say much while riding. We would often go long distances without him saying a word. He was very contemplative.

I was in college. He talked a great deal about education and the need for it among Black people. It was his belief that education was one of the main avenues which the race would have to travel in order to gain upward mobility. He felt that this was the single area in which Black people had to channel their energies.

Reverend King had a love for history. One Sunday he used the famous General Napoléon Bonaparte in his sermon. While driving him to the parsonage after church, Reverend King said: "I really admire Napoléon and his ability to analyze a situation, organize, and get to the root of the problem quickly." I do not recall Reverend King ever getting angry. He was slightly disturbed with me once. I had his 1954 blue Pontiac. I was supposed to take it to the parsonage. Instead I drove the car to the campus. I parked it and decided to go to my dormitory room and take a nap. I do not know how long I had been sleeping, but I heard a knock on the door. I opened it and Reverend King was standing before me. He had an afternoon engagement and no mode of transportation.

"What happened?" he inquired.

"I fell asleep."

I gave him the key and he departed. Reverend King did not get angry. I was not dismissed from my duties.

Reverend King loved cake. One Sunday someone gave him a cake at church. To my surprise he gave the cake to me.

"Take this to the campus," he said. "Share it with the other boys in the dormitory."

Reverend King was a very humble man. When he was not in the eye of the public, his demeanor was the same.

I successfully completed my studies at Alabama State College and moved to Cleveland, Ohio. Reverend King came to speak in Cleveland in the 1960s. I went to hear him. He recognized me and invited me to attend a dinner with him in a private home that evening.

Mrs. Hazel Gregory

The movement had been going on for about three months when I started working with the MIA. Initially the organization met at First Baptist Church, where Reverend Ralph Abernathy was the pastor. The organization moved from the church and started meeting at the Baptist Ministers Conference Building on Dorsey Street. Events necessitated a third move and the MIA relocated to the Citizens Club owned by Mr. Rufus Lewis. A fourth move put the organization in the Black Bricklayers Hall. The overseer of that building was Mr. Percy Doak, who was a member of Dexter.

One of the earliest donations the MIA received from outside the State of Alabama came from New York. Mr. Bayard Rustin brought the money to Montgomery in a big brown bag. Reverend King said: "Hazel, I never saw so many dollar bills."

I was one of several secretaries for the MIA. Mrs. Erna Dungee (Allen) and Reverend R. James Glasco were the financial secretaries. Mrs. Jo Ann Robinson headed the organization's newsletter.

One of the things that impressed me about Reverend King was that he honored his commitments. For example, Dr. Adam Clayton Powell invited Reverend King to come and speak at Madison Square Garden in New York. Reverend King had already committed himself to his friend Reverend Bennett in San Francisco. Reverend King went to San Francisco and sent Mr. E. D. Nixon to speak at Madison Square Garden.

New Yorkers took up a large donation that evening. Mr. Nixon said there was so much collected until the monies were put in tomato crates and stacked.

Money from outside of Alabama started coming in to support the movement. Local residents came up with creative ways to raise money. Mrs. Gilmore testified on Reverend King's behalf and was fired from her job at a local restaurant. Two clubs were later started. The clubs sold sandwiches and dinners. They vied to see which could turn in the most money. Mrs. Gilmore was the leader of The Club From Nowhere on the Eastside. On the west side of the city was The Friendly Club.

People from across the country sent Reverend King money. Countless checks came in to the MIA headquarters with "Pay to the order of Dr. Martin Luther King, Jr." Regarding the checks with his name on them, Reverend King's standard statement was: "Give it to the movement."

He never accepted the checks. The movement was his major concern.

There were ten Black banks across the South into which the organization put its money. Two banks were in Atlanta, one was in

Nashville, with the rest in other locations. Mr. Nixon would sometimes take money when he made one of his train runs and make a deposit along the way when passing through one of the cities where one of the banks was located.

There was a financial board that handled the organization's money and kept records. I still possess most of the records. Reverend King never handled the money.

Station wagons were purchased to help transport the supporters of the bus boycott. There was a Black car dealer in Tuskegee and some of the vehicles were purchased through him.

One of the things that helped during the movement was the espionage work of Black domestics in white households. They often telephoned the MIA office and told us what was being said and planned in the white community. Household conversations were repeated to us. Sometimes maids would stop by the MIA office on their way home from work and divulge information. Their information was valuable, accurate, and timely.

It is not publicized but white people also kept the movement informed of the plans of the white community. There was a white gentleman who was sympathetic to the cause. He kept us apprised of anything that was potentially harmful. This individual had to leave Montgomery in later years.

There were white people who would give Black bus boycotters rides. For example, there was a Mrs. Folmar who used to pick up her maid each morning. Whether going or coming, if Mrs. Folmar saw a Black maid going to work, she would give the individual a ride.

Mr. Nixon became frustrated and separated from the movement before the bus boycott ended. He started a voter registration group and took many of the young people with him.

Many domestics, maids, and common laborers lost their jobs. They had no regular incomes. Their stand for right had become very costly. The MIA used much of its money to help these committed supporters. Mrs. Rosa Parks became a paid employee of the MIA. Her job was to fill out applications for people who needed financial assistance to pay light bills, water bills, electric bills, and other necessities. A committee would review the applications and mail checks.

The organization tried to do the same for professional persons who were terminated from their jobs for supporting the movement. The professional people had skills and could move on to other states and procure employment. Before leaving, a meeting would be held sometimes and a big collection taken. The money would be divided between those who were leaving. It was a parting gift of sorts.

There was a trial at which several MIA workers were supposed to testify. Erna testified first. She was asked about MIA monies. I was called to testify. I prepared to go forward. As I was getting ready to move, reporters and lawyers rushed in and said: "The bus boycott is over."

I did not have to testify.

Celebrities started coming to town. They usually stayed at Mrs. Irene West's home. If not there, with the King or the Abernathy families.

It reached the point where the police were participating in plots to stifle the movement. Their participation was discovered.

There was a white cab company named Red Cab. Cars from this company had been seen in several communities where bombings had taken place. Black residents learned that when a Red Cab was in the neighborhood there was likely to be trouble.

I received a call in 1957. Three foreign students were in Arkansas and wanted to visit Montgomery and inquired about a place to stay. One student was Indian, another African, and I cannot recall the nationality of the third. They had a white guide. I agreed to meet them at the train station.

I telephoned Erna (Dungee Allen) and told her what was going on. She drove to the train station. We greeted the four men. As we greeted them, I saw a red cab. The driver left his parked position and drove swiftly past us.

"We are going to jail tonight," I told Erna.

"What makes you say that?"

"I saw a red taxi."

A short distance from the train station three police cars and a motor cycle cop were waiting for us.

"Get out," one of the policemen instructed Erna. "Give me your driver's license."

He looked at it. There was nothing to charge Erna with so the police took the four men. We followed them to the police station. Each man was taken to a separate room and interrogated. They knew nothing of value to reveal.

I told the authorities: "I will take them to Mrs. West's house for the night."

Reverend King enjoyed good food. He liked the food at Kats Diner. Kats Diner could cook pig ears like no other. At night we used to order dinner, sit, eat, and talk about how afraid we were.

Reverend King left Montgomery. He asked me to come to the church and help him pack up some of his belongings in preparation for leaving.

After Reverend King left Montgomery, things began to gradually erode. The preachers said they were tired of it all and were returning to their traditional ministries. Some who were involved in the movement became ambitious. The voting booths the MIA had, to train people how to vote, were taken by an individual and claimed as his own.

Many white people came to work with the movement. I felt that some were government informants. I remember a lady coming to the MIA office and spending a considerable amount of time in this community. I saw her on television in 1994 and recognized her. She admitted on the show that she worked for the government.

Reverend King returned to lead the Selma to Montgomery March. I was at the MIA office on the last day of the march and was going out to meet the marchers. Reverend H. H. Hubbard came by the office.

"Are you going to join the marchers?" I asked him.

"I will sit here and watch the office, if you want to go," he said.

Maids continued to keep us alert. Moments before I left the building a maid called and said: "Get word to Reverend King. A car (she gave the description, such as the color, make, model, year, but I cannot recall the details) is coming from Birmingham. The men in the car plan to kill Dr. King."

She heard the plan over a two-way radio where she was working.

I contacted one of the men at Saint Jude and asked that the information be passed on.

I later learned from a white insider that indeed the men who were to kill Reverend King that day were in Montgomery when the rally was held in front of the State Capitol. However, the authorities made arrangements to guard against disruption.

After the Selma to Montgomery March, Mrs. Viola Gregg Liuzzo came to the MIA office. She was a white woman from out of state. She and a female friend were preparing to return to their home state. Mrs. Liuzzo first wanted to take some young Black marchers back to Selma which was their home. Mrs. Liuzzo's friend said: "I will get our things ready so we can depart when you return."

A call came into the office from Hayneville, a small town just before Selma. I said: "Mrs. Liuzzo, a message just came in from someone in Hayneville. The person said the Klan is waiting for you. Don't come back."

Mrs. Liuzzo said: "The children cannot be left here. We must take them back to Selma."

Mrs. Liuzzo left Montgomery and dropped the young marchers off in Selma. She was killed returning to Montgomery.

These are just a few recollections from the era of the movement. I hope to write a more detailed account one day.

Index